D1579000

GEOGRAPHER

THE DESCENT INTO MADNESS

Ad Gridley

Michael Terence
Publishing

First published in paperback by
Michael Terence Publishing in 2018
www.mtp.agency

ISBN 9781912639137

For my brother

THE

GEOGRAPHER

THE DESCENT INTO MADNESS

Ad Gridley

FOREWORD

For anyone who is dealing with the life changing effects of mental illness, be it first hand or otherwise, this honest and personal account will encourage you to see that there is hope.

My brother is one of the one in seven who reacts so severely to the use of a drug commonly available in all towns and cities across the UK and beyond. I sincerely miss the brother I grew up with but deeply admire and love the brother he is now. I implore you to laugh at the funny parts and cry at the sad. More than anything, I truly hope you can learn what the human mind is capable of creating, fighting and ultimately overcoming. With the correct help and support, mountains can be overcome.

MEDICATION

Quetiapine, marketed as Seroquel among others, is an atypical antipsychotic used for the treatment of schizophrenia, bipolar disorder, and major depressive disorder. It is also sometimes used as a sleep aid due to its sedating effect, but this use is not recommended. It is taken by mouth.

Common side effects include sleepiness, constipation, weight gain, and dry mouth. Other side effects include low blood pressure with standing, seizures, prolonged erection, high blood sugar and neuroleptic malignant syndrome. In elderly people with dementia its use increases the risk of death. Use during the latter part of pregnancy may result in a movement disorder in the baby for a period of time after birth. Quetiapine is believed to work by blocking a number of receptors including serotonin and dopamine receptors.

Quetiapine is primarily used to treat schizophrenia or bipolar disorder.

Very common (>10% incidence) adverse effects. Dry mouth, dizziness; headache; somnolence (drowsiness; of 15 antipsychotics quetiapine causes the 5th most sedation. Extended release (XR) formulations tend to produce less sedation, dose-by-dose than the immediate release formulations.)

Common (1-10% incidence) adverse effects. High blood pressure; orthostatic hypotension; high pulse rate; high blood cholesterol; elevated serum triglycerides; abdominal pain; constipation; increased appetite; vomiting; increased liver enzymes; backache; asthenia; insomnia; lethargy; tremor; agitation; nasal congestion; pharyngitis; fatigue; pain; dyspepsia (indigestion);

peripheral oedema; dysphagia; weight gain

Rare (<1% incidence) adverse effects. Sudden cardiac death; syncope; diabetic ketoacidosis; restless legs syndrome; hyponatremia, low blood sodium; jaundice, yellowing of the eyes, skin and mucous membranes due to an impaired ability of the body to clear bilirubin, a byproduct of haem breakdown; pancreatitis, pancreas swelling; agranulocytosis, a potentially fatal drop in white blood cell count; leukopenia, a drop in white blood cell count, not as severe as agranulocytosis; neutropenia, a drop in neutrophils, the cell of the immune cells that defends the body against bacterial infections; eosinophilia; anaphylaxis, a potentially fatal allergic reaction; seizure; hypothyroidism, underactive thyroid gland; myocarditis, swelling of the myocardium; cardiomyopathy; hepatitis, swelling of the liver; suicidal ideation; priapism, a prolonged and painful erection; Stevens-Johnson syndrome, a potentially fatal skin reaction.

Neuroleptic malignant syndrome, a rare and potentially fatal complication of antipsychotic drug treatment. It is characterized by the following symptoms: tremor, rigidity, hyperthermia, tachycardia, mental status changes (e. g. confusion), etc.

Tardive dyskinesia, a rare and often irreversible neurological condition characterized by involuntary movement of the face, tongue, lips and the rest of the body. Most commonly occurs after prolonged treatment with antipsychotics. It is believed to be particularly uncommon with atypical antipsychotics, especially Quetiapine and Clozapine.

Discontinuation. Quetiapine should be discontinued gradually, with careful consideration from the prescribing doctor, to avoid withdrawal symptoms or relapse.

The British National Formulary recommends a gradual withdrawal when discontinuing anti-psychotic treatment to avoid acute withdrawal syndrome or rapid relapse. Due to compensatory changes at dopamine, serotonin, adrenergic and histamine receptor sites in the central nervous system, withdrawal symptoms can occur during abrupt or over-rapid reduction in dosage. However, despite increasing demand for safe and effective antipsychotic withdrawal protocols or dose-reduction schedules, no specific guidelines with proven safety and efficacy are currently available.

Withdrawal symptoms reported to occur after discontinuation of antipsychotics include nausea, emesis, lightheadedness, diaphoresis, dyskinesia, orthostatic hypotension, tachycardia, insomnia, nervousness, dizziness, headache, excessive non-stop crying, and anxiety. Some have argued that additional somatic and psychiatric symptoms associated with dopaminergic super-sensitivity, including dyskinesia and acute psychosis, are common features of withdrawal in individuals treated with neuroleptics.

Citalopram (brand names: Celexa, Cipramil and others) is an antidepressant drug of the selective serotonin reuptake inhibitor (SSRI) class. It's used to treat depression, panic disorder, dysthymia premenstrual dysphoric disorder, body dysmorphic disorder and obsessive-compulsive disorder.

Adverse effects. Sexual dysfunction is often a side effect with SSRIs. Specifically, common side effects include difficulty becoming aroused, lack of interest in sex, and anorgasmia (trouble achieving orgasm). One study showed, however, when remission of major depressive disorder is achieved, quality of life and sexual satisfaction is reported to be higher in spite of sexual side effects.

Citalopram theoretically causes side effects by increasing the concentration of serotonin in other parts of the body (e. g. the intestines). Other side effects, such as increased apathy and emotional flattening, may be caused by the decrease in dopamine release associated with increased serotonin. Citalopram is also a mild antihistamine, which may be responsible for some of its sedating properties.

Common side effects of Citalopram include drowsiness, insomnia, nausea, weight changes (usually weight gain), increase in appetite, vivid dreaming, frequent urination, decreased sex drive, anorgasmia, dry mouth, increased sweating, trembling, diarrhea, excessive yawning, severe tinnitus, and fatigue. Less common side effects include bruxism, vomiting, cardiac arrhythmia, blood pressure changes, dilated pupils, anxiety, mood swings, headache, and dizziness. Rare side effects include convulsions, hallucinations, severe allergic reactions and photosensitivity. If sedation occurs, the dose may be taken at bedtime rather than in the morning. Some data suggest Citalopram may cause nightmares.

Withdrawal symptoms can occur when this medicine is suddenly stopped, such as paresthesia, sleeping problems (difficulty sleeping and intense dreams), feeling dizzy, agitated or anxious, nausea, vomiting, tremors, confusion, sweating, headache, diarrhea, palpitations, changes in emotions, irritability, and eye or eyesight problems. Treatment with Citalopram should be reduced gradually when treatment is finished.

———

In the summer of 2005 my daily prescription was **300mg Quetiapine** and **10mg Citalopram**.

THE RAMPAGE

I don't need the pills

The last time I went without my medication for longer
than four nights, I was arrested, briefly jailed and
admitted to a mental hospital. It should have been the
wake-up call I needed, but no. It was August 2005. I'd
been excelling at martial arts and singing and I was
losing weight at a healthy pace. These successes sadly
made me complacent. How could some smug,
supercilious doctor half my age profess to know more
about my mind than I did? So, angrily, I weighed things
up and threw out all my Quetiapine and my Citalopram
pills.

Toasting my reflection

The first signs of relapse came fast and loud. I began
drinking at a pub I'd never been to before. It was quite
busy with a mixed, Friday night crowd. I've never been a
big drinker, but still I kept ordering beer after beer. Now
and then, I'd also ask for a whisky. I had to get
thoroughly wasted. I didn't talk to anyone but the
barman during this time. There was a large mirror
behind the bar, and I remember my reflection coaxing
me on. I kept raising toasts to myself in it. They were
some of the most devil-may-care things I could've said
out loud. My toasts would be:

"My friend, you are one beautiful mother fucker!" and
"Here's to the toughest c**t in London! The world is
yours!" Each time, I'd solemnly raise my glass to my own
reflection. Then, I was being physically pinned to the
floor. I was on my back looking upwards through a load

of arms and legs. I think I'd started a fight, and then the whole pub had jumped on me. The next morning, I woke up in a hospital. Remarkably, I only had some slight bruising. I got paranoid after that, quickly got dressed and found my shoes and ran all the way home.

Kissing strangers

The next night, still refusing my meds, I went to another town where I had no friends. I walked up to a couple in the street - they must've been about my age. While the boyfriend looked away, I moved in and grabbed his girlfriend. I dipped her low and kissed her full on the mouth. The boyfriend turned back - he was furious. He started swearing, yelling and pushing me. During all this, I chose to count to myself how many times he pushed me. I counted twenty-two, but still I didn't respond. I think I just smiled and straightened up again each time. After those twenty-two pushes, he lost interest. I wandered off after that and got the bus home.

Tearing my clothing

The third night without my Quetiapine and Citalopram, I this time headed in to central London where the rampage really got going. It was a hot, summer's night. I was wearing jogging bottoms, a T-shirt, trainers, but no socks – which I usually would wear. I had no pockets, so I kept my flat keys, cigarettes and lighter in my hands the whole time *a virtual stranger had given me this. The lighter was red, green and white like the Italian flag. This alone would've got my mind racing, but the man who gave me it had had psychotic episodes in the past. I thought I was now personally protected by the Mafia because of the lighter. Just before I left for London, I posted my 9/11 commemorative issue of the Sunday Times Magazine through his letter box as payment.* I had my Freedom Pass tucked into my shoe and I was ready for anything. I caught a bus to somewhere random in east London. I bummed cigarettes off strangers. I shared a joint with a man in a record shop. I finished off any old can of booze I found and at one point, I even got down on the floor and drank from a rain puddle. Then I thought arachnids were mocking me. Not any one spider, more like *every spider on the face of the earth.* In retaliation, I'd find one in the centre of its web and burn it until it scurried off to the edge. Then, I'd laugh and run off to find the next one. Unusually, I was feeling a lot of hatred that night. To let off steam, I tore my clothes. I loved the sound of the tearing and then the new feeling of cold air.

Munching coffee beans

And so, I kept moving. I loved the rain, and loved being rained on. I started thinking that the doctors had put me on meds just to hold me back. How could a stranger tell me what was going on in *my* head? This was the real me. The doctors were trying to stifle my potential. I went in a random coffee shop and sat down with my drink. I started bawling my eyes out for no reason. This went on for ages. So long, in fact, that I soon felt embarrassed and left. I went to another coffee shop after that and found a customer quietly reading. There was no-one there, just the two of us. I saw some stairs leading downwards, so I walked past the "Staff Only" sign and followed the stairs down. There was nothing there, so I came back up. I walked up to the till, grabbed some raw coffee beans and started munching them. I then added more and more beans without finishing the first mouthful. After a few more handfuls, I had hundreds of coffee beans all in my mouth. I went outside where some workmen were digging up the road and spat the coffee beans into their hole. They started yelling at me, so I ran off. At a safe distance and out of sight, I ripped at my trousers. Then I lit a cigarette and started aimlessly walking again.

Ejected from the betting shop

When night-time came around again, the streets were changing around me as I walked. The buildings I'd just walked past had swapped places with new ones. All the heavy magic was meant so I'd lose my mind –The Geographer exercising his temper. Then, I found a betting shop with solitary gamblers. On the floor under the plasma screens showing horse-racing I started crawling about on the floor. I was really acting out, but no-one seemed to notice. Maybe they were yelling at me. Someone might have called the police. Either way, I didn't notice them. I left soon after.

I surrender my house keys

Next, I split up my two flat keys – one was a Yale type key and the other to double lock. I left one on a doorstep in Stratford, and the other one miles away on a doorstep in Kensington. I didn't know the people at the addresses, but I trusted in The Geographer enough to leave them where I did. This carelessness demonstrates that I wasn't thinking of returning to my flat at all. When I finally had to return, it took me ages to change the locks. I felt compelled to allow the two keys' new owners to locate me and bring about my whirlwind new life of luxury and leisure. The following morning, the households probably just threw the keys away.

The trendy pub

Then, I found a pub called The George Bush. I had no idea where I was. My Dad had always been quite vocal about George Bush's policies – both George W Bush and his father. Ever since my catastrophic gap year, I'd wanted to redeem myself in my Dad's eyes. Attacking this George Bush pub seemed perfect. So now, about four or five days without my medication, I went in the inflammatorily-named pub, ready to hate everyone in there. The place was heaving with trendy drinkers. There were brown and white sugar lumps in bowls on the bar. They didn't have real edges like regular sugar cubes do, either. I put a brown one in my mouth and sucked on it, regarding the sugar as sustenance. I wasn't even hungry. Then I decided I'd gathered all the calories I needed and put the rest of the wet sugar lump back in the bowl. I didn't notice anyone watching me, but I was in a world of my own. I went back outside to the night rain to consider my next move.

I plan my attack

I wanted to throw a brick through one of the pub's windows. I was supercharged by a want for my father to be proud of me (although in reality, he'd have strongly disagreed with my actions). It was the George Bush ideology I was attacking, not the drinkers. I didn't want to hurt anyone, so I chose the window facing the condiments trolley. The brick would smash the glass and land harmlessly amongst the cutlery. I was breathing hard now. I took a half-brick from the builders' rubble and focussed on the condiments window. I hefted the brick in my hand, ran up to the window and threw that brick as hard as I possibly could.

Toughened glass

It turned out the window was made of toughened glass. The brick just bounced off. I was stunned and disappointed. And, glued to the spot: I was fascinated by all the new cracks I'd made. I stood there watching it for an eternity. In a heartbeat, I was thrown down onto the floor, prevented from leaving by the people who'd rushed out of the pub. I wasn't resisting at all, though, not struggling. In fact, with my free hand, I began moving and scratching the gravel on the pavement. I was now relishing the sounds of that.

Handcuffed and arrested

After a few minutes, the police arrived, 'cuffed me and put me in their van. As we drove, I brought my legs up through my hands, leaving them instead 'cuffed around my front. Then, reality dawned: what did I hope to gain by demonstration of suppleness? Chances were, I'd be compliant when they opened the doors, anyway. So, a little sheepishly, I climbed my legs back through the 'cuffs and sat like they wanted me to until we reached our destination.

The man with the slicked back hair

Now, I was in a cell somewhere. It felt like it was underground. I was in conversation with a smartly-dressed man with slicked-back hair. We were talking in hushed tones about something very legal. I had no idea what was going on. I made noises here and there, just to show willing. He finally gave me some important papers and left. I went to the bench at the back of my cell. I saw all the Government letterheads, carefully folded up the pages into paper planes, returned to the cell door and threw them out through the bars. They glided silently into the corridor. I smiled because they'd floated so far.

Banging in the prison van

I was brought before a tall desk where I was asked for my papers. I didn't have a clue, so they decided something for me. The next cell was noisier, but I still had it to myself. You could hear a great deal of laughing, wolf-whistles and slamming doors. And at some point I was led, again in 'cuffs, to a prison van. I had just enough room to sit down, but I could see the outside world (traffic, people, buildings) through the purple window, in a cubbyhole part of the van. I heard banging coming from the person in front of mine. I couldn't see him, but still I started banging in response. Both of us were trying to out-bang the other, louder and louder. Then, the guard had tolerated enough and hit the doors loudly with his stick "Stop that banging!" When he said that, we both burst out laughing.

Rats armed with lasers

In my new cell, I was also alone, so I threw the mattress on the floor. I could see the CCTV camera watching me from the corner of the ceiling, but so what? There was a dirty toilet, too. The seat had long been broken off and not replaced. They gave me beans and scrambled eggs. I was grateful for the food. After that, I was in another cell with a big, wooden bench along the back wall. I thought there was a sewer pipe running just underneath the bench, and it was full of rats. The rats had lasers strapped to their backs. Whenever I sat on the bench, I felt the lasers firing at me. Along with the rats, there was a gruff, smoker's voice and it was continuously talking about me. It could have been The Geographer, it could have been a deputy. I was informed about all the pain I had coming to me. To help me cope with the terror, I loudly burst into song. After a few minutes singing/screaming, the jailers gave me a cigarette. I'd totally forgotten that other people would have heard me. I stopped singing and enjoyed the smoke. They took me out of the cell and told me I was on remand. I had to wait in prison until my court appearance. One of the guards farted loudly and all the others fell about laughing.

Strip searched

I was strip-searched. There was nothing invasive, but I got the feeling that there could have been if I was too cocky. I probably looked too ill to want to smuggle anything anyway. Then, they gave me some grey slacks in exchange for my rags. I appreciated the clean clothes. It seemed like echoes were calling my name. I'd hear my name from the left and look to the left, when, in fact, someone from the right was calling me. I didn't know what was happening. Then I just thought: "You're relapsing. Just try and relax."

The prison welcome pack

And I was sat down in someone's office. There I was given a small bag of new supplies and a piece of paper. In the bag was a little pouch of tobacco, papers, a prison-issue cigarette lighter, a pack of mints and a bar of chocolate. When the guard left briefly, I hid the chocolate and mints under different piles of paper on the desk. I thought these two items would later act as bribes. When the guard found them, he'd think "Aha! This man remembers his friends!" and I'd be given a TV in my room. Nothing like that happened, of course. All I did was pass up the chance to eat both the chocolate and mints myself. On the paper was the PIN number I'd need for my outbound phone call from the wing. The PIN number was about twenty digits long. They told me I could use it when I was in the main prison hall during free flow. While the guard was still gone, I noticed a tiny spider crawling on the PIN number paper. I was still so consumed with hatred for spiders that I burnt my PIN number as well. I heard the guard coming and quickly hid the smouldering paper. I sat there as nonchalant as I could manage when he returned to the room. Luckily, he didn't bring it up and told me to go back outside.

Purple cotton

They gave me fresh bedclothes to take to my next prison cell. I was the first one there. I went straight to the long piece of purple cotton someone had woven around the bars in the window. It looked like someone had put a lot of thought into those patterns. I imagined one wrap around two bars meant one night, one wrap around three bars meant your girlfriend came to visit, that sort of thing. It felt like there was magic in those threads. I quickly unravelled it all. Then, I wrapped the thread in between the bars just how I'd like it - I'd infuse it with *my* magic. Looking through the bars, I could see hundreds of pigeons on treetops and buildings. I'd heard prison time sometimes was called "bird". Maybe it's because of all the pigeons? It's probably just that some birds are kept in cages.

Big Russian cellmate

My cell mate was a tall Russian and he took the bottom bunk. He'd been arrested with some friends after a massive, drunken brawl somewhere. They'd effectively invaded a pub. It was the Russians against the locals. When the police arrived, everyone who hadn't run off was arrested. I read and explained his legal paperwork to him and things seemed amicable. Just when I was thinking I'd lucked out with a friendly cellmate, my tobacco went missing. I was lucky not to be raped.

Free flow

Free flow happened twice a day. During free flow, people made phone calls or played ping pong or pool. I still had racing thoughts and was feeling feral - so I went exploring. I was nosing around that prison wing like I had a film crew with me. Downstairs in the main hall, other people were playing ping pong. Some were real athletes. I suppose it was better than fighting. I wandered up to the pool table. The person holding the pool triangle played next. I was holding the triangle and I felt relaxed and ready to play. Then, the prisoner who'd just lost snatched the triangle from my hands. He was easily twice my size, so I wasn't ready to argue. I walked off, slightly bemused. If I was thinking at all straight, I wouldn't have lined up to play in the first place.

Looking over your shoulder

I thought that looking over my left shoulder was a sign
of weakness. If I looked over my right shoulder, I'd be
left alone. If I forgot about the idle lefts, I could always
reset things by quickly looking over my right shoulder
again. In prison, it was doubly important that I use only
my right shoulder for any glances backwards. These
were the things occupying my mind.

Load up on rolls

After a few hours locked in our cells, we were released
again briefly to get food. A silver line of hot plates and
servers down the centre of the hall had appeared where
the pool tables had been earlier. Dinner was casserole,
boiled carrots and mashed swedes. Everyone also each
took about four bread rolls. Dessert was a small pot of
strawberry trifle. The cell doors were kept open until
everyone had finished eating. When you'd finished, you
left your plate just outside your cell.

Just say no

The next night, I was in a different cell. The cell mate I
met there was firmly established. It was like an
Aladdin's Cave full of different sugary and sugar-free
cordials. He generously offered me anything I liked from
his collection. Then, about half an hour later, he wanted
me to do heroin with him. I told him no. He went ahead
alone anyway. Then, he became paranoid. He destroyed
the table, the chair and threw all his bedding on the
floor. He even pushed over his cordial bottles. I lay there
watching him from my bunk. He seemed to be leaving
me alone. Straight after he'd finished banging and

crashing and loudly destroying everything in the cell, about half a dozen prison officers burst in through the door. The Ribena-drinking heroin-smoker then feigned terror and ducked out the door past them. He blamed everything on me, saying that *I* was the monster! Next thing I know, I'm ordered down off my bunk and carried bodily out of the cell. From there, I'm carried downstairs to receive my punishment: solitary confinement.

I'm about to be nuked

Things were bleak in my new cell. Everything was concrete: the bed, the sink, even the stool by the sink. The floor was a blood red/brown colour. And the shouting and laughter from the other prisoners was louder. Of course, the cell door slams and I burst into song – really screaming the high notes. They'd put me here for being wild, so I thought I'd act that way. Then, they brought me the prison chaplain, plus bodyguard. He was a dodgy holy man. When he left, I thought he'd subtly performed the last rites on me. I was about to be killed. Prime Minister Tony Blair and his deputy Gordon Brown had a nuclear bomb-proof bunker near my cell. They'd sent a state-of-the-art robot along the corridor outside towards me on little track-tyres. It was armed with a powerful laser. Then, Tony Blair and Gordon Brown fled their bunker, leaving behind the nuclear bomb. All the other prisoners had been quietly evacuated during this tense time, leaving me to be killed. Terrified, I threw myself flat on the floor, right up against the side of the concrete bed. In this prone position, the concrete bed frame would shield me slightly from the explosion. Then I waited for the bomb to go off.

The holding cells

Next, I found myself in a holding cell with some other
people. I think we were getting ready for court
processing. I got chatting to the man next to me. He was
a cab driver. His drunken fare had tried to pay him with
a chip he'd won earlier at a casino. My friend then
repeatedly demanded proper payment and, ultimately,
he'd had to use the baseball bat he kept in his boot. My
friend was well-dressed, while I was back in my rags.

The English courtroom

Next, I remember standing in an English courtroom. I
stress "English courtroom" because it's quite different
from an American one. Everyone was wearing wigs, as
you'd expect, but each person in the room was standing
at their own level corresponding to their status. The
judge was at the very highest level. Everybody else –
lawyers, note-takers, spectators – all stood at various
levels below the judge and above me. And I was standing
on the bottom level, almost as if I was in a pit.

Looks can be deceiving

It was a fearsome room – what with all the dark,
hundred-years-old wood panelling and bad lighting. I
could imagine the judge shouting "Take him down!" at
some point. Luckily for me, he didn't. After a while
rustling some important papers, one of the women (also
in a wig) said:

"This isn't your first time in front of us, is it [my name]?"

I told her that it was. It looked like I'd been set upon by
bears, so I could see why she'd think that. Then, they
charged me with criminal damage. Behind me was a

glass panel through which I could see both my parents.
That was when the gravity of the situation hit home. I
remember wondering if my Dad understood I'd attacked
the pub because of him. I've brought it up since, but it's
not a pleasant memory for either one of us.

Outside again

Everything was soon settled and forms were signed.
Extremely relieved, I found myself outside in the
sunlight again. The plan was that I be returned to the
safety of a psychiatric ward. So, scruffy as I was, I had a
cigarette, and chatted with my parents. When the
ambulance arrived, I was pleased that they let me smoke
inside, although it wasn't strictly allowed. Visually, I
was still a mess. I probably needed a shower, too.

The lighter swap

Whenever I've been hospitalised, I've always been made
to feel welcome. As the years came and went, I got to
know the nurses and trust them like old friends. Also,
they provided me with all the toiletries I needed - even
clothes at one point. My bed will have been freshly-made
with clean sheets and covers and I had access to the
patients' pantry. The pantry meant unlimited food and
coffee, tea, chocolate and milk. If you were polite, the
nurses would even lend you money for tobacco, which
was easily the highest priority item. Your unspoken
initiation to the group came when you swapped lighters
on the coffee table with another smoker. The new patient
arrives in the smoking room. They'd swap lighters
(silently and discreetly) and they'd be accepted. The
other person uses your lighter from then on, and vice

versa. Oftentimes, I'd recognise a few of the other patients. Then, those people would introduce me to the people I didn't know and we'd all keep smoking. I should really have swapped my lighter with the group before getting cleaned up that time. My backstory would've had more gravitas if they'd seen me as a pub damaging wanderer of the streets. If I'd shown up all hairy, stinky and with clothes torn, though, it would have been harder to be discreet with someone else's lighter, so, maybe it was for the best. There in the open hospital, both sexes can mix together freely in the main public areas. Also, you can carry mobiles and lighters with you.

Trail of destruction

So, I cleaned myself up and got into a fight. Nurses arrived before it got too bad, though. I walked into the pantry after that. Soon, I found myself looking at the floor. I'd just torn a cupboard door off its hinges because I couldn't find the Weetabix. Then, I'm hurling a jar of peanut butter at a window to watch it smash for no reason. No-one wants to sit near me now, so I finish my smoke and walk into the dining area. I see a cleaner there putting a curse on me with her eyes and then the ward's table-football game hits the floor around me. While I'm making sense of the wreckage, someone tells me my Dad's on the phone. I walk up to the phone and accidentally knock over the man standing by the phone. He yells something and nurses restrain me for the second time. They're not happy with my behaviour. Before I know it, I'm being relocated to a closed (high security) psychiatric hospital. This is uncharted territory.

Pocket swaps

While I was being driven in the back of a police van to
the new hospital, I had an idea. I had to swap over all
the things I had in my jeans pockets. Everything in my
right-hand pockets (keys, cash, tobacco) had to be
switched with the things in my left and vice versa. It was
essential – as if I wasn't already confused enough.
Another thing I had to do on that journey was to throw
myself about heavily from one wall of the van to the
other. When we arrived at the closed hospital, they
allowed about half an hour for me to calm down a bit
before opening the back doors and grabbing me. Once I
was past the main three security doors, I had to turn out
my pockets and they searched me again. They took my
lighter, shoelaces, belt and phone (this they put in their
safe). A nurse had to watch me for that first 24 hours so
I didn't kill myself. Visitors were also watched closely.
They had a rule about no ex-patients visiting current
ones, and at least one of my own visitors was searched
for explosives.

FIRST TIME AT A CLOSED HOSPITAL

Sharp scratch

I walked out into the main dining area. It was music
therapy in full swing. One of the nurses was also a house
DJ. He had his authentic vinyl record decks out and was
skilfully mixing songs together while everyone else
danced. I'd seen people use decks like these before, so I
thought I'd give it a go. Of course, I'd never actually done
it before, but I'd always thought it was easy. So, I
basically barged in (after being watched for 24 hours)
and put my hand on the record that was playing. I
scratched that thing slowly and noisily for what seemed
like a good fifteen inches or so, right across the record.

New music therapy

This was not how it was done. Straightaway, the music
stopped playing, and the patients stopped dancing.
Everybody, including the DJ in charge and all the
patients dancing, stared at me in shock and anger. I
permanently damaged the needle with that one motion.
In the space of ten seconds or so, I'd managed to damage
some costly equipment and I'd mugged off a whole room
of mental patients - before I'd even had a chance to meet
them. Perfect. After that, music therapy was different
part of my illness meant that I couldn't always
understand someone else's feelings. I could offend
someone with a fairly simple insult, and not know firstly,
that I'd offended them, and secondly, that I'd paid them
an insult. As far as I was concerned, the people dancing
before I ruined their fun had totally exonerated me
almost straight away. If they had a problem with me
after that, it was them taking it to heart. It was never my

*fault. Although I was never attacked after that, I think
one of those patients had taken a shine to me – although
it was an all-male ward - and had vouched for me
somehow. Soon after, I made a friend of one of the
tougher patients who was present during the nasty
scratch, only years later did I realise that maybe that's
what'd happened.* Now, it meant that we had to sort
through a big box of old CDs. We each chose a track we
wanted played and the rest of us scored that track out of
ten. There was now no dancing (and, sadly, for me) no
learning DJ skills. To keep the peace, the chocolate bar
prizes came thick and fast.

Hostage nurse

One of the other patients smashed the mirror in his
room. He attacked a nurse with one of the shards. He
was yelling that he had to be freed. After a while, the
nurses managed to talk him down. Because of that
attack, we all had our mirrors removed. We had to shave
looking in the shiny, brushed steel parts of the doors
instead. Patients using razors were watched very
carefully and usually also timed.

Awkward door handle

This first stay of mine was before the 2007 nationwide
smoking ban. There was a smoking/TV room in the
closed hospital where someone always had a James Bond
film on video ready to watch. You could only properly
open the door to this room from the outside, where there
was a regular door handle. The only thing you had on the
inside of the door was the small, round handle part,
without the lever. If you were at all claustrophobic, it
would have caused a panic attack. Of the dozen or so

people on the ward, only one person could consistently open it by himself. He'd often show off about that. The rest of us, if we were stuck in that room, would have to get someone's attention from outside just so we could leave the room. The whole door handle situation seemed like an intentional wind-up for most of us. Formal complaints always fell on deaf ears.

Out of tune guitar

One of the other patients had been arrested for climbing trees in a town centre. He wanted to eat the berries in the top branches. Now on the ward, he'd play us songs on his guitar. It was so out of tune. I used to say you could strum it just once and play every known chord. I tried for ages to tune that thing, but it seemed to be beyond tuning. He could play it himself with no problems and that's what really mattered.

The mouthwash incident

To break the monotony, I tried smuggling some alcohol onto the ward. Each morning, all the patients got together for the group shopping list. We wrote down what we wanted, paid the nurse, and they brought us our things. Commonly requested items were tobacco, lads' magazines or chocolate; for the flush amongst us, it would also be soft drinks and small cigars. First step of my plan: I started publicly moaning about having gum disease. There were already many hypochondriacs on the ward, so my moaning was par for the course in that place. After a few days of this, I casually wrote mouthwash on the list. Given all the complaining I'd been doing, no-one thought it strange. When the shopping arrived later that day, I was over the moon. I took the Listerine back to my room and necked half the bottle in one go. Immediately, I felt lightheaded. It was strong stuff, but the taste reminded me of the dentist. I considered my getting hold of it a success, but I didn't do it again. I learned soon after my smuggling that it was possible to get mouthwash on prescription. While it was free, you were only given a tiny amount – nowhere near enough for any real effect.

Glimpses of bus adverts

If you had leave to the closed hospital garden, staff took the added precaution of jotting down what you were wearing. Security was tight. To get to the garden, there were first two heavy doors to pass through. The inner door was controlled via a nod from the nurse to the control room. For the second door to open, they made you stand with your nose to the opposite wall. The nurse with you then tapped in the special PIN number. Beyond these doors, there was a quiet corridor with a tuck shop that was great for junk food. At the end of this corridor was reception and, to the right was the garden. It was great just to see the local buses drive past. Over the tall perimeter fence, you could catch glimpses of the adverts for films and products that had just come out, or for holidays. Even just a quick peek at one of those signs made you feel a bit more human again. These are all things people "on road" can take for granted. After weeks of nothing but the smoking yard, the green space of the garden was really refreshing.

Keep it safe

We all had little safes in our bedrooms. We got to choose

the six-digit PIN number ourselves. I used to store Sony minidiscs in mine. My Mum used to bring me dozens every time she visited. Then, it dawned on me that no-one else there even had a minidisc player – so why would they take my albums? So, I started keeping food my visitors had brought in (chocolate, olives, pistachios) in the safe instead. As my leave increased, I thought I should keep my tobacco in the safe instead. It was much more likely to get stolen by another patient. I was very fortunate that nothing severe happened to me while I was there.

Patterns of discharge

Ward round happened once a week – on open and closed hospitals alike. Doctors only seemed to stay for a few months at a time, but we all knew you had to impress them. They could grant you more leave and then discharge you. The exit path for all of us patients went like this:

> • Discharge from the closed hospital put you back in the open hospital
>
> • Discharge from the open hospital put you back into the community.

IN THE OPEN HOSPITAL

The staff treat us to a takeaway

So, a brand-new, purpose-built hospital had just been completed nearby. We were all taken there by minibus. It was strange to see that even the nurses were excited. It was to be our new home for however long our doctors deemed necessary. When we arrived, we went exploring. Everything was brand new. In one of the clean, white baths, there were some little bits of plastic the builders had left behind. In the old hospital, your bed was secured with some curtains. Here, the bedrooms came with doors, and locks on those doors. There were a couple of double rooms, but I landed a single one. To celebrate the first night, the nurses treated us all to a Chinese takeaway. It was before the smoking ban, so we stayed up all night, excited and chatting in the spotless smoking room. There were two rules to follow. Both applied from the stroke of midnight:

- The patients' pantry was locked; and
- The TVs were switched off

Every night, since the usual drinks were out of bounds, the nurses put two jugs of cordial on the lunch counter for us. Then, we had virtually the run of the place until morning.

Warm and cosy smoking room

I have some good memories of insomnia in the hospital during the years before the smoking ban. We'd stay up all night just for the hell of it. Sometimes, it felt like we were on a school trip. It was a chance to shoot the breeze with someone in the same boat as you. On a good night, the smoking room was brilliant. It was warm, full of smoke (which helped keep non-smokers away), and its door was never locked – except for the twenty minutes per day when it was cleaned. As the night wore on, the nurses began to venture away from the control room less and less. This room was around a curving corridor and about 30 yards away. The lights were turned down at a regular time each night so the corridors would be only dimly-lit. This was when we came alive – bearing in mind that we'd slept all day. If someone had alcohol or weed (which was more available than I thought) now was the time to start sharing it out.

Is a beige brain good?

Late night conversations could get a bit strange, but they could also be magical. After the TV had been turned off, I was sitting across the room from another chain-smoker. This lady also seemed to be still too hyped-up to sleep. She was from Eastern Europe and always used to roll her *r*s with relish. I was just considering how she sounded when, out of the blue, she said:

"Heyyy! I can see yourrr brrrain frrrom heeerrre. You haaave a beeeige brrrain, you dooo. Eeet ees beeeige".

Me: "Thanks".

Then, for a while, silence piled up around us.

"My boyyyfrrriend has rrreached his aaaerrroplannne".

I considered this statement carefully... I didn't know the man, where he was going or why, still:

Me: "Is he armed?"

Her: "Yesss. He eees verrry well arrrmeddd".

Her boyfriend's happy

A long while passed where we just smoked and said nothing. She had lemon cordial; I had orange cordial (the pantry was long closed). Her breathing was laboured, but things were relaxed. Then I said:

"Has he landed yet?"

Her: "Yesss. Heee eeesss happy".

I really thought we'd been reading one another's minds that night. After we spoke, I went to bed and forgot about it. Years later, I started wondering if I actually did have a beige brain. Then, I gave it some more thought, and put the whole episode in a box in my mind marked "Insane: do not touch". There's enough paranoia in the real world to worry about, let alone extra.

The badly bruised lady

For the biggest impact on arriving, you wanted to be brought in by the police, and maybe still yelling and covered in blood. I remember one lady came in like this. She had a broken leg, bruises all over her and one eye was totally bloodshot. It turned out she blamed the police for her injuries after she'd trashed a corner shop and resisted arrest near her house. She was very generous: always offering a roomful of people each a cigarette. But, of course, you never wanted to be in her bad books.

Hiding from his dealer

At the other end of the respect spectrum, there were people who were in the hospital in hiding. Richard was one of these people. He owed Alex (his dealer) a great deal of money and now he's being hunted. Alex knows

Richard lives with his parents and he's found the street, but doesn't know Richard's house number. Now, Richard's curtain-twitching and pacing about and letting Alex's calls just go to voicemail. His parents are getting worried. While Alex is just outside getting angrier – Richard has a plan. If he scares his parents enough, they'd think he's relapsing. Then, he'd be admitted to hospital and he'd be safe from harm. While in the hospital, he could save up the money he owed Alex – and all the while he'd get his board and lodgings free.

Richard attacks his parents

So, Richard turns on his mum and dad. The way he described it, (beaming with pride as he recounted his story) he hit his mum in the head with a fruit bowl, which made her start screaming. Then, he pushes his way through to the kitchen to get a knife. Then, he wrestles with his dad who winds up getting stabbed in the hand. Then, he heads out into the garden. His parents are convinced that their son is relapsing now. Meanwhile, Richard is having the time of his life, destroying whatever he can find in the shed. He knows he's now put a little extra distance between himself and the car out front (Alex is now thinking of knocking on doors to find his man). And all the while, Richard's yelling out phrases to guilt-trip his parents *"You never loved me enough, you're rubbish parents. All I wanted was a normal life! You two are selfish cowards that you should live through me. What about my feelings?! What about me? No more problems from Richard. Oh, no. You've always been embarrassed about me – I wanna kill myself! I'd rather rot in hell than hear one more of your stupid ideas. Mum, you should have had me aborted. The last vestige of any control over your cursed son! (I'm paraphrasing, but he really was a nasty piece of work, this Richard).* They can hear someone outside angry in their car, but now, Richard's banging and crashing in the shed. Richard's parents call the police. They explain that their son's attacking them and needs psychiatric help. Then, after lying to the PEAT (Psychiatric Emergency Assessment Team) doctors about how paranoid he is, Richard gets admitted to the hospital.

Still unashamed

While he's in hospital, he's safe as houses and soon saves up the money to pay his dealer. The plan worked like clockwork. He would often burst out laughing whenever he told his story, thinking about how easily he manipulated the system and his parents. Soon after they'd been attacked by their only son, they gave him a top-of-the-range boom box to use while he languished in safety in the hospital. I'd like to think that Richard's since changed his ways, but I'm not sure he has.

Shots fired!

At the opposite end of the scale, along with the lady with the bloodshot eye, was Ian, an ex-army bodybuilder. He was part of an elite group instructed to guard the Prime Minister (his articulate language and decisive manner added credence to this). His story began when he was at a top-level army briefing, and his commanding officer had gotten angry with him. He was so incensed that he'd got out his gun and shot at Ian's desk, missing him by inches. Although it was meant as a warning, this was reckless behaviour. Ian reacted automatically – as per his training. The other soldiers who held Ian back probably stopped a man being killed that day. The commanding officer who'd shot at Ian's desk was rushed to hospital with several broken ribs, a broken arm and a concussion. And Ian had been admitted to the same hospital as me. On top of this impressive backstory, he was built like a juggernaut.

Melancholeric people

(I must admit I created this word. Melancholeric means being simultaneously sad and angry)

I've seen quite a few otherwise fearsome people having to wait for simple things on arrival at the hospital. It was like they'd been generals in the army, but now they were bombardiers. They'd have to wait in line for hours for something like an interview with a doctor, or they'd have to wait for their phone for their allotted, weekly talk-time. These patients took anger and sadness to new levels. They'd usually just stare straight ahead or at the floor. The police who'd brought them in would often hang around, just in case the nurses needed their help. The patient would by this time have tested the patience of the authorities so much that no-one was taking any further chances. The law would be quoted to them *"Sir / Ma'am, you do realise that under the Mental Health Act 1977, we have the right to force medication on you? Due to your recent destructive actions, you have been deemed unsafe for free circulation in society and you'll be detained here at this mental institution until sufficient behavioural progress has been observed. If you resist the administration of said medications, under the Willful Refusal of Medications Act 1983, you will be overpowered, rendered unconscious and said medications will be then administered directly into your veins." Or words / dates to that effect* to make them surrender their rucksack, take some sedatives, or to even just get out of a chair. As things grew quieter and more menacing, the psyched-up nurses would now be four or five deep, the new patient remaining seething but silent. This person would come into the smoking room for the first time after such a dramatic entrance and it felt strange. It was much like feeling a heavy bass note thud in your chest, but without the music.

No cocaine

I had leave to the shops with Ian once. He wanted cocaine, but we got thrown out of all the pubs we tried. As we walked back to the hospital, Ian got spooked and started applying dirt to his face. He was worried because we were being watched from across the road. He said he'd seen the sun glinting off a sniper's lens on one of the roofs. This was paranoia at its finest and who was I to say he was wrong? Crucially, he hadn't realised that the dust he was using was too dry to darken his face, so he was getting nowhere. I wasn't ready for this. The plan was to have gone to the pub, had a few beers and returned to the hospital before our curfew. We'd eat breath mints to cover the smell of booze on our breath as usual. I was worried now. My weight-lifting, guitar-playing, former-soldier friend was having battlefield flashbacks. Squatting behind a bush, he wanted to go and find this sniper, overpower him and extract information. I hated having to desert a friend, but I couldn't see his idea of storming the house going at all well. I ran back to the hospital without him and went straight to my room. I discovered the next day that when Ian had returned to the hospital, he'd been so violent that the staff had given him the liquid cosh and put him to bed. I'm glad we didn't get hold of that cocaine; it could have been a whole lot worse.

Make *them* wait for *you*

Whenever a nurse called you, for a meeting or something, something we patients sometimes did was to try and make *them* wait for *you*. They'd call you for a meeting, see you were smoking a cigarette, and say "Could you come through when you've finished that?" Then, you'd finish that cigarette and defiantly start another one. It was a bit churlish, but it seemed like we were always being made to wait for them. To us, this attitude was payback. Obviously, if you dragged it out to like twenty or thirty minutes and they're still waiting for you, they'd cancel the meeting and you'd have to sit around and wait for another whole week. Apart from the bounteous food available, it was easy to feel unimportant, overlooked and invisible. If numerous funding cuts for the NHS were the trigger, patients and their visitors waiting ages (with their complaints falling on deaf ears) was the fallout. With luck this situation will change.

Sumo palm prints

I'd read somewhere about the Japanese sumo. Fans in Japan queue up for ages for an inky sumo palm print, instead of an autograph. During the signing sessions, the sumo first thumps their hand on the ink and then thumps that inky hand onto the stack of paper. An underling would take the palm print away and the sumo thumped the ink again - ready for the next one. The sumo palm prints were then distributed to the fans. I thought this was great. It was just before the London 2012 Olympic Games and I really wanted sumo wrestling to be included as an official Olympic sport. I thought that it hadn't been included because the IOC (International Olympic Committee) was racist. So, I launched a personal campaign to make it an official sport. My approach was to tell everybody I met about this travesty of justice: even other people's visitors and the ward round doctors. Then, I'd perform a silent, sumo demonstration for them – a tribute to the pre-match routines I'd seen them do. I'd raise my leg to the side at head height and stamp down that leg hard onto the floor. Then, I'd repeat it with the other leg. All the stamping soon made it painful to walk. My campaign had lasted for all of three days. Much later, I read that the Japanese don't consider sumo wrestling a sport, it's far too sacred for Olympic medals. I should really have researched it better before I hurt my feet.

Cheryl might detonate

So, I was waiting just outside the PEAT offices because I felt ill again. Just ahead of me to be seen was Cheryl, and she was more worried than usual. She was opening doors and going through them. Then, after the door had closed, she'd turn around and go back through it again, and so on. I could hear a loud, sustained noise - one I'd never heard before. I was sure it was the utterly unique sound of a bomb about to go off, which chimed with Cheryl's panicky demeanour. I quickly surmised that she had the bomb with her in her rucksack and that she was a suicide bomber, however reluctantly. The bomb she had would be detonated from afar. She'd been told to meet me at PEAT that day and destroy both of us along with that part of the building and some doctors. Now I was in danger. I calmly moved from where I was and sat on the third stair a little way off. From this position, I'd be safely shielded from the blast due to the small concrete wall in between us. I prepared for her to explode. After a short (yet very tense) wait, Cheryl was summoned by the PEAT doctor and I was seen soon afterwards. No bombs went off that day. I was admitted to the hospital at the time, but I haven't seen Cheryl since.

Snoopy and Woodstock

Once I get a destructive thought in my mind, it can take a long while for it to be dismissed. I'd be lying on my bed, listening to music through my earphones in the dark with the curtains drawn. I used to call it "Snoopying," but, it's daydreaming. I approached the music like it was an ancient mystery. I saw the music as a supremely powerful thing – often listening to an album from start to end before I got up and had another smoke. I wanted to preserve an imagined treaty between myself and the music's creators. I'm a lot like Snoopy during these times. In the Peanuts cartoons, you'll often find Snoopy lying on his kennel. His little, yellow bird-friend Woodstock (named after the famous music festival?) was always flying nearby. If the red kennel starts flying, Woodstock would follow in a random pattern close-by. While all the talk of Snoopy may seem harmless, I would be quietly ruminating on some of the most harmful thoughts I've ever encountered. Of the six or so serious suicide attempts I've had, most were linked to the periods when I was daydreaming. Daydreaming like this is now something I never do.

Hammer and nails

So, I was daydreaming in hospital – and this chapter is
not for the faint-hearted. I was working for God. I was a
holy assassin. All the targets had been preselected by
God, which was reassuring. I had to knock a nine-inch
nail through the target's head –using a floating
hammer– to kill them. First, a (somehow tangible)
hammer and nail appeared next to the victim's head.
Then, on God's count, I'd twist my torso so violently to
one side that the force generated transferred from me,
through the hammer, and into the nail - and into the
head. If the timing was precise and the force extreme
enough, I'd "see" the target slump to the floor, dead. God
would say "So-and-so lies dead". Straight after a kill,
another victim was lined-up - and I'd feel guilty and
alone, lying on my hospital bed.

Don't fail God

Apart from when I was twisting about in my bed
thinking all this, I also heard God's booming voice
whenever I looked in the mirror. I could hear him
persecuting me. He'd say things like: "There he is. That's
our man... Get a good look at him!" I could also feel
spirits and ghosts soaking up the details of my
appearance. There were always different people visiting
the ward: health professional, friends of patients. It
would've been easy for a hitman to visit, catch a glimpse
of me and kill me once I'd been discharged. When I heard
those voices watching my reflection, this was God's
safety net. He was ensuring all the other holy assassins
knew what I looked like, in case I spoke to anyone about
these killings. All I could do was continue being a holy

assassin. I'd learned that a weak twisting could result in the nail being hit only half the way in. Also, if the timing was out, God couldn't add his crucial blessing to the kill. I felt terrible whenever I messed it up: I'd failed God (triggered his murderous rage) and I'd denied the target a painless death. I really couldn't understand it - when in my life had I been so evil as to deserve this torment?

The new trainers stare down

Even in real life, God was on the ward with me - and he was belligerent. He'd often stand up close to the TV and stroke the side of it whenever a good-looking newsreader came on. His appearance was always messy. He used to sleep rough on the streets a lot, and it looked like he still did. One afternoon, I found him sitting in the smoking room face-to-face with Dean, one of my friends. Both men were sitting just feet from one another, staring at each other. Apparently, the homeless Bulgarian had stolen Dean's new trainers while he was asleep. He'd crept into his bedroom and lifted the shoes from right beside the bed – the two hadn't even spoken before this event. The shoes were worth around £130 and Dean was furious (and slightly impressed). Being a thief or a liar in a hospital can often lead to violent reprisals, so this was a strange development. The old man was still wearing the shoes. You could sense the respect one had for the other. It was the old versus the new, maybe even rich versus poor. They sat there in silence, motionless. They weren't even smoking, which was quite unusual. Other people came in the room, had their cigarette and left. All the while, the two men sat there staring. They parted amicably after that, but that standoff seemed eternal.

God says do press-ups

Another time, God commanded me to do twenty press-ups. I was in a packed smoking room at the time. I heard Him say "do twenty press-ups, perfectly, straight away". I assumed everyone else had also heard the message. So, I politely, but quickly, made some floor space where I could do the press-ups. I did them as perfectly as I could. My life depended on it. I knew that if I disobeyed His command, I'd get a thunderbolt in the head and flung down to the bottom layer of hell to suffer forever. If I think I'm hearing any commands like this these days: I'm ready. I reply to that thought by asking: Well, where would it end? Or, I'd remember that it's a slippery slope. If you concede to these thoughts even a little bit, what follows that? What if they ask you to attack someone or burn something down? Over the years, this vigilant thinking has kept me from doing far more stupid things than I've done. Voices like that really don't deserve any contemplation. Still, after I completed God's twenty press-ups, no-one in the smoking room batted an eyelash or stopped smoking. Once I'd gotten my breath back (which seemed like ages), all we could hear again was the sound of the TV and of lighters and/ or matches being struck.

Self-harm with ceramics

In the hospital, for the safety of the patients, dangerous items were confiscated at the door. If you were in one of the observation rooms, belts and shoelaces were also removed. Glass or ceramic cups were considered dangerous, too. I thought confiscating ceramics was a bit over the top, until I witnessed something. I was in the smoking room when another patient came in and almost dived at the trespassing ceramic mug on the coffee table. Without a second's thought, she smashed it down on the wood floor. She quickly found the biggest piece and began carving into her wrists – the lines soon bringing up blood. Luckily, the nurse watching her managed somehow to stop her doing any real damage. I was stunned. I've felt desperate myself before, but I'd never seen it so badly in someone else.

Self-harm with a scalpel

One man I met was into self-harm. It was the only way he could get rid of the stress he felt – it helped him relax. He'd managed to find a proper surgeon's scalpel to cut with. Sure enough, his cut-up arms all showed fresh, angry scabs and scars. They were so violent they wouldn't ever fully heal. He treated the mesh of red like a gory badge of honour. I got the impression that he wanted me to jealous. I couldn't tell him what I was really thinking.

Banter in the smoking room

Unlike when you meet a normal person, patients in the hospital would often bring up intimate things to complete strangers. We'd openly discuss unusual secret things we'd done, our partners, suicide attempts and the strength and type of meds we were on. This was small talk for us. Although it was usually a subconscious thing, these confessions could be a way of competing with the others in the room – who's had the worst life. There'd be stories about the highs and lows of bipolar disorder, or run-ins with estranged family or the law due to schizophrenia. If I'd just started a visit to the hospital, I'd walk in to a room full of mental patients smoking. It would be the start of yet another time in the hospital ten's quite a lot of residential visits for any one person. This was the number of spells on the wards it took for me to learn my lessons. Changes had to be made to my lifestyle – namely, stopping drinking so much and ruling out completely any recreational drugs. This also meant recalibrating my social circle. These changes then led to epiphanies which then meant I could shrug off my old life and start making my loved ones feel proud of me again. Then, we'd start talking about suicide, like I said, or mildly criminal activities.

Peer pressure to smoke

In the past, I've even made my way to the hospital by myself. I'd have a PEAT interview and get admitted. Even though I might be some weeks or months without smoking, using gum and nicotine patches at the time, I'd still buy cigarettes and a lighter on the way there. I've tried to resist the lure of smoking with everyone else on the ward, but the willpower it takes has always been beyond me. On the wards I've been on, there's just nothing else to do. Cigarettes were a good ice-breaker in a roomful of strangers. I'll always associate mental illness with smoking.

He lives in a fortress

One of these times, a man who'd just arrived was telling the rest of us in the smoking room about how he'd tricked the police. He'd thickened and triple-locked the front and back doors to his house. Also, he'd installed steel bars and triple-glazing on all the windows. All this was because the police had had to force entrance so many times in the past. He also thought the police had hidden a tracker device on his van at one point. So, the police wanted to arrest him and had been forced to camp outside his house for days. They'd tried to break down the door, but couldn't get through his security. After a good few days of this siege, our friend finally ran out of food. What with also his poor Dad on a megaphone, he came out quietly. After that, they arrested him, gave him some food and threw him in hospital which is where we found him.

Geoff, the slow smoker

Geoff took ages smoking. He was a pot-bellied sixty-year-old with a bald patch and a stoop. He'd saunter into the smoking room with his cigarette and lighter in different hands. Maybe there'd be a cheeky look sideways (to someone who didn't get the joke) but aside from that, he said nothing. He'd sit down on his own and begin. Very slowly, he'd rest the cigarette in his mouth. Then, he'd bring the lighter up to meet it and light the cigarette. He always kept the flame held to the lit end of the cigarette once it was lit almost as if to make sure it was alight. After he took his first drag, he'd let the smoke dribble slowly out of his mouth, much like a cigar smoker would. Before long, his routine really riled a lot of us. Soon, Geoff began hating me back which gave me an idea.

Man vs. dinosaur

Geoff and I had crossed paths in the past. He'd been a diplodocus and I'd been a caveman. I'd hurled a rock at his dinosaur head back then in the Jurassic Period and it had killed him. When the other cavemen heard about this, they'd killed hundreds more and soon succeeded in making diplodocuses extinct. No wonder Geoff was upset with me! A good while afterwards, I learned that cavemen and dinosaurs never lived simultaneously on the earth. It was a relief to hear that – I like the idea of dinosaurs.

Rival gangs

There was a news item about a fatal stabbing in a tower block quite nearby. They reported the name of the victim, and one of the girls in the smoking room quickly stubbed out her cigarette and left. Then Dean made a phone call. A few minutes later, I left Dean to his conversation and went out to the pantry for more coffee. The girl who'd left the room earlier was also on the phone –yelling at someone. It transpired that both belonged to the different gangs involved in the stabbing. Later that evening, Dean switched at the nurses - throwing chairs and things. Turns out it was one of his friends who'd been stabbed that day. Except for the liquid cosh, lorazepam was the strongest sedative the nurses in the hospital could use. One lorazepam would send most patients to sleep fast. That evening, they'd given Dean *four* lorazepams. Never had one person been given so many at once. Even after they'd given him all those sleepers, he was wild and crazy for a good hour after that.

The aggressive germophobe

The girl who left the room after the stabbing had a real problem with germs. If someone the other side of the room sneezed or blew their nose, she'd jump up from her seat and start screaming.

"What d'you think you're doing? You trying to kill me?" then she'd open a window really wide, even if it was freezing outside.

"You know those germs are gonna reach me! I should have you killed! Behaviour like that." Then, she'd either kiss her teeth and noisily push a chair away. Usually, the person who'd sneezed would be scared stiff and start apologising. One time, I even saw her order the person out of the room.

"Just leave. Leave!"

Watching the Grand Prix

I saw this same girl, calmer now, holding court another time in the smoking room. She came out with some real whoppers, and seemed convinced of every word. We were in the smoking room, watching the Grand Prix.

"You see that car?" pointing to the latest McLaren. "That one!"

We all noticed the car.

"I designed that car. That colour scheme? Mine. All those modifications? Mine. Even the tyres."

She'd then sit back in her chair as we tried to make sense of her claims.

"Three years at the Sienna Institute of car design I spent. Those bastards stole my plans! I came up with that design. The lines on that roof? All mine. They owe me. Big time!"

Octuplets

Also, she'd tell everybody she'd been pregnant with octuplets. As if this wasn't enough, she was now telling us that she'd given birth to *two* sets of octuplets. If any young men came in to see her on visits, they were always introduced as her sons, girls were always daughters. Bearing in mind these visitors always looked dangerous, no-one ever questioned her. Patients in those hospitals could be a little naïve, and usually would believe anything – me included. For years, I thought she was Bruce Lee's daughter – which is what she'd said. She had slightly oriental eyes, and was quite beautiful. At the time, Bruce Lee was my role-model, so I always paid his daughter a lot of respect and I'd make her coffees, just in case.

Fruit touchdown

I thought of a new way of letting off steam. There was a fruit bowl on the lunch counter that no-one ever touched. I took one of the apples and gathered my anger. The plan was to throw an apple at the wood floor. After I'd double-checked no-one could see, I stood in the middle of the dining area and hurled that apple. It splodged on the floor, where it left a little tuft. The rest of it reached out in a huge circle on the floor like a firework. I was really pleased that bits of apple had made it into all corners of the room. Straightaway afterwards, I acted casual. I felt superhuman, but I didn't want to be the one to tidy it up. This was the only time I threw an apple, mainly because I felt guilty about the mess.

Art critic

There were a few things to which I've never owned up. One of those things was breaking the glass on a piece of art. It annoyed me whenever I walked past it in the corridor. I was feeling angry with something and thought it'd be great to elbow the painting as hard as I could. So, I did. The glass smashed, but I remained there to watch. A nurse heard the smashing and asked me what I was doing. Even though I liked that nurse, I lied and said I'd found it already broken. I was told to move along and soon enough the handyman repaired it.

24hr handyman

The handyman was always on call. With him around, no pane of glass, toaster or kettle would stay broken for long. This efficiency was important because of the message it sends. Seeing destruction can lead to people destroying more things. At the very least, broken things can make you feel more depressed. Whatever the reason, and whatever the hour, the DIY needs of the hospital were always swiftly met. There was always furniture or kitchen appliances getting destroyed by angry patients.

Ambient malaise

I could never really relax in the hospital. There was too much unease and interpersonal disconnect. One minute, a given patient would be sobbing; next minute, they'd be whooping loudly. Then, they're giving you all their tobacco and then they're threatening to kill you. This was the main reason I chose to daydream so much – although this was really just swapping one type of tension with another. Generally, the criminals in there would warn others not to take a photo of them. It was entirely possible for some of these characters to have real people baying for their blood. I soon told people not to photograph me, either - but only really to blend in. Whenever the walls were officially being painted, the workmen were observed with great suspicion by some of the patients. Those patients usually thought the workmen were spies for enemy's crime families. The knock-on effect of the paranoid patients feeling invaded led to other patients being suspected. Then, that patient would be attacked and they'd retaliate. Then, their families would visit and retaliate, and it all went around and around.

Strangers watching me

I had a problem with strangers in the hospital. I thought everybody was spying on me. At one point, I thought they were working specifically for my ex-girlfriend. Why she'd bother, I'll never know - she'd finished the relationship with me. While we'd been together, she'd asked me if I'd like to be in the Mafia. I'd said no, but later, I'd be thinking about exactly how powerful she was. She'd sent killers into the hospital to get me. At the time, any stranger who walked past slightly too close, or who looked at me for slightly too long would give me panic attacks.

Can people on TV see out?

I was watching some live TV in the smoking room. They'd just put a number onscreen for viewers to call if they wanted to win a prize. Whenever they asked people to call the number below, this poor girl would jump out of her seat and start yelling.

"No! You can call me! Yes, it's Sarah Jane Swift! Yes! No! I'm more important than you! No, you call me. It's 07 (insert her number)... Why won't you call me? I'm important! Why won't you call me? I put you where you are now! I've always watched this show. How can you be so ungrateful? I know you can hear me. Why are you ignoring me? It's Sarah Jane Swift! Why are you being so cruel?" By this point, she'd be in floods of tears. Sarah Jane Swift got like this during all the live shows: I'm A Celebrity, Get Me Out of Here…, X Factor, The Voice, all of those shows. It was a heart-breaking to see her plead with the presenters every time. Internally, I think we all wanted them to talk back to her. I'd heard her reel off her phone number so often that it was seared into my brain for weeks.

Early morning orange juice

If you were unlucky, you had meds in the morning - at 8am. Breakfast was at 9am. Breakfast meant either Weetabix, Bran Flakes or Cornflakes. Also available was brown or white toast with little packs of margarine, butter, jams, Marmite, etc. All these foods were always in the pantry anyway. The only difference was orange juice, which was limited to one beaker per person. If you really liked orange juice (and if no-one else showed up for theirs) then you could have their ration as well.

Up early on Saturdays

Saturday morning meant a cooked breakfast, if you could get out of bed. In your dressing gown, rubbing your eyes, you'd walk into the main dining area and there'd be a line of breakfast foods all waiting up at the lunch hatch. Like with the juice rations, if no-one else got up, you could go back for more servings. There was scrambled egg, toast, baked beans, bacon and sausages. It was delicious and it made you feel a bit more normal. It was hearty food and, of course, no money had changed hands.

Once you'd eaten your fill, you'd then have a cigarette and go back to bed.

Lunch

Soup and sandwiches were served every day at noon. The soup was different depending on the day of the week, but they all tasted similar. The sandwiches came in different flavours, though: cheese and tomato; tuna; ham and tomato; egg mayonnaise; prawn; chicken mayonnaise. None of them contained butter or margarine. To spruce up your sandwich, you could always add some brown sauce, or just dunk the sandwich in your soup. Most patients would take an extra pack of sandwiches from the counter and sneak it back to their room. Once you were safely in your room, you could eat them whenever you liked – if no-one came in and took them. Usually, the nurses put about a dozen packs of sandwiches on the lunch counter for people to take. Almost immediately, they'd vanish. Hospital could be a desperate place.

My stash of luxuries

At any one time, my windowsill would be a treasure trove of all sorts of goodies. I hid everything behind those curtains. The cleaners probably knew about my stash, but why would they care? Highly-prized items would include: toilet paper on a roll, multi-packs of crisps and chocolate bars, Radox bath foam, coffee. Also, I'd have tubs of coleslaw, margarine, pistachio nuts and, of course, the free sandwiches from lunchtime earlier. Sometimes, you'd miss the nurse when they'd left for the official shop of the day. If that happened, you had to sweet talk another patient – with leave to the shops – and then they'd buy you what you wanted.

Creating history

Sometimes, I'd have no visitors arranged to come in and I'd feel fine. Other times, even if I'd just said goodbye to a visitor, I'd feel lonely. Depending on how it had gone, I'd dwell on the cup and spoon they'd used while we'd been talking or playing cards. I'd make sure no-one touched those things. I'd pretend to myself that they'd only gone to the bathroom and that they were coming back soon. Other times, I'd set up cups and plates in such a way that it looked like a visitor had come to see me when no-one had. I called it "creating history".

Objects of desire

People with no leave would need all sorts of things from the shops. Popular items ranged from batteries to make-up, margarine to cranberry juice, soft drinks to roast chicken, and everyone wanted tobacco. Luckily for us, there was a big supermarket not that far away. The first time I was given unescorted leave to the supermarket was like I'd been exhaling for hours and now I could breathe in again. I had money in my pocket, I was hungry, and I was surrounded by delicious, affordable foods. If I wanted a treat, and a change from the free dinners, I had my favourite homemade meal. This was: a ready-roast chicken, coleslaw and some crusty rolls. I'd take these ingredients back to my room and, somehow, eat the whole lot in one go (my stomach capacity has since shrunk). Also, I'd get pistachio nuts for snacking.

Creature comforts

I also always made sure I had proper toilet paper in my room. In every bathroom in the hospital, all that was available was thin, little squares of paper. There was a box of this toilet paper on the wall, but you needed three sheets just for one wipe. Often, you'd find these boxes torn off the wall, broken by whoever was in there before you. Other necessities were margarine and proper, caffeinated coffee. Strictly speaking, you weren't meant to have glass jars with you, but if you were crafty, you could sneak them past the staff.

Black market items

For the right price, there was always someone willing to smuggle booze into the hospital for you. In the park, you could empty out half a bottle of lemonade, or some other clear liquid, and top it up with vodka or rum. Or, you could empty out a 1l carton of juice, and top it up with the alcohol. Once, I smuggled in three small bottles of alcohol. I had one of vodka, one of whisky and one of rum. It was going well, until I got caught. What gave me away was the empties, which were just as incriminating as if you'd had full ones. At the time, the thought hadn't even crossed my mind that I'd get caught. It seemed OK to me to just put the used bottle into the bin in my room. The cleaner found it the next day (she couldn't really turn a blind eye to that) and the nurses suspended my leave. After that, if I bought more alcohol, I made sure to put the empty bottles somehow in public bins. If this wasn't possible, I'd smuggle them out of the hospital when I was next on leave.

Ward round

Waiting for ward round was a big part of life as an inpatient. Even if your CPN (Community Psychiatric Nurse), your Mind advisor, your partner and your family were all with you, you could still be kept waiting for an hour or more. Typically, you'd walk in the ward round room and find the seat meant for you (furthest from the team assessing you and nearest to the door). The people already present would include (at least): the all-powerful psychiatrist, an OT nurse and a ward nurse. For about twenty minutes a week, it was all about me. I felt like I was famous – but without the money and legions of fans. Often, I'd sit there in ward round nodding, smiling and answering questions *during these times, my mind would be racing. I'd be thinking about the nurses there and why they're moving their feet like that; I wonder if those two are sleeping together; why doesn't that bloke look up – has there been a death in the family recently? I bet she got stoned last night; these people only work with the mentally ill to distract from their own illness; he wants a pay rise; she is really sexy, I wonder if she has a boyfriend, or girlfriend? – all kinds of stuff, but on the outside: "So, how are you feeling now?" "Fine, doctor. Thank-you." To be fair, he's paid to catch you out, so it's not always this easy to get distracted.* But, straight after the meeting, I could remember no details of what was said. Even though I was listening out for the vital announcement of leave, my mind was still a blank. It was crucial that someone attended these meetings with me, so I could learn about what had just been decided and, often, what I had myself said.

Typical questions

Ward rounds were serious meetings, but sometimes I played-up. During one of them, the doctor asked me:

"Can you hear any voices now?"

I'd say:

"Only yours, doctor".

I remember thinking this witticism was a win for me. Other things they asked would be things like:

"Do you feel safe here?"

And:

"Are you having any intrusive thoughts?"

Confession leads to observation

Broadly speaking, the questions the doctors asked me were designed to test my sanity. Oftentimes, I'd feel safe again quickly, but now, I was bored at remaining locked up. The only real way of getting discharged was to tell the doctor what he wanted to hear – of course, it helped if it was true. Most admittances, after a short time shitting myself in the real world (more often than not after having gotten comprehensively stoned), I'd confess everything to a PEAT doctor. Due to the extent of my mental situation, they'd be forced to admit me – usually for at least two weeks. After that very first interview, the staff had to be doubly sure that I'd pose no threat to myself or others if was discharged. Time's a great healer, but it can't be rushed. If I was discharged prematurely, then killed a lollipop lady or something, the doctor would be held accountable. After each hospital stay, I'd find that the daily meds I had to take would include some new neuroleptic drugs. If no other drugs were added, then the quantities of the existing ones would have been increased. Also, having someone professional to discuss nightmares with was also very helpful. What made the doctors so cautious was that I would often be a drastically different person once I'd regained my sanity. Unfortunately, the temptation to smoke that next joint was often too strong to resist.

Still cocky

I'd heard of patients throwing chairs at their doctors during ward round. Nothing good ever came from attacking your doctor. Sometimes, I'd be bored and act up a bit during ward round, but nothing serious. I thought they'd only give me a tiny bit more leave anyway, what could go wrong? I remember once they asked:

"How would you say you're feeling today? If you had to put it into words."

My reply was:

"I'm feeling euthymic, doctor".

I'd seen the word euthymic used in letters about me between doctors. If happy faces have a smile, and sad faces have a frown, a euthymic face would have just a straight line for a mouth. In doctor jargon the euthymic patient's mood was neither high nor low.

Christmastime

Christmas in the hospital was surprisingly exciting. Even with no alcohol, no friends and no family, it still seemed to work. The first sign Christmas was coming was the streamers that appeared throughout the ward. They must've been put up while everyone was asleep. It was great to see fancy things for Christmas. As Christmas Day drew closer, tables covered with buffet food appeared. It was the first time I tasted a prawn from a prawn ring. Also, there was chocolate cake, chicken drumsticks, sausage rolls and, of course, small sandwiches in triangles. I was blown away.

Auld Lang Syne

To wash it all down with, there were half a dozen 2 litre bottles of fizzy drinks. Because of the location and the people involved, there was a fair amount of greed about. Although there seemed to be plenty available, it was still every person for themselves – honour amongst thieves was out the window. Immediately after the staff had revealed the food and left, the best crisps were spirited away. I saw people take them and return to get more. I knew I had to do the same myself or I would go without. So, I took the salt and vinegar ones while I could. Soon after that, all the beef ones went. And after that, all that were left on the table were Twiglets, plain crisps and cheese niblets. Come New Year's Eve, we all stayed up to see in the New Year. We all smoked and watched the concert from The O2 Arena. On the stroke of midnight, we linked arms and sang Auld Lang Syne, then went to bed.

Free kebab

There was a man with me in the hospital who took quite a shine to me. He always called me "Beckham!" He's the only person I've ever met who thought I looked like David Beckham. He used to have doner kebabs delivered to me for no reason. I loved the kebabs, but was too naïve to understand what he might want in return. Earlier on in his stay, you'd see him stumbling around the hospital, naked but for a bed-sheet. This man was married with three kids. I think his wife felt enough shame for all of them put together.

Dinner

Dinner time was 5·30 pm. It was the same every week: Tuesday was fish, Thursday was curry, that sort of thing. It was no Saturday breakfast, but it was a free, hot meal. Nearly everyone would rush back to the hatch to get seconds and thirds. I knew I was getting fat, so I tried to avoid the puddings. We were feral when we ate in the hospital. Often, you'd hear a patient ask for seconds or thirds –just because it was free. At the time, we thought we were milking the system. People would want seconds or thirds of the main course, or dessert. Then, their visitors would bring in sweets and crisps on top of that, or a McDonalds meal with a big milkshake. Outside of set meal times, of course, there was always the pantry. If you had the cash with you, there was also the vending machines - or a massive takeaway. The small fruit bowl really doesn't even get a mention. The oranges were crap and the apples were sour. Apart from my secret touchdown earlier, the fruit always stayed there keeping up appearances.

Pizza deliveries

Like I said, we sat down to eat at 5:30 pm. Even if we had then had seconds, we were hungry again by nine or ten. These are the times when talk of takeaway food deliveries began. The mood was electric when that happened. The choices were varied: pizza, Chinese,

Indian or kebabs (at my flat, I couldn't call out for takeaways – delivery riders were getting hijacked for their pizzas too often for that). Pizza was the best choice for a group order. Once the pizzas arrived, they'd be divided-up between those who'd chipped in. Of course, the pizzas could be half one topping, half something else. We always went for the biggest size we could – so "extra-large" every time. There were two reasons for this: firstly, it was better value; and secondly, while you were wolfing it down in front of everyone, you felt like The Daddy. There were six stages to enjoying a pizza from the hospital:

- First, you'd choose which pizza crust and which toppings
- Second, you'd place the order – usually from someone's mobile
- Third, there was the wait while it was being cooked
- Fourth, the hospital's doorbell would ring
- Fifth, the patient with the cash would pay the delivery man – plus tip.
- Sixth, there was the eating

The thrill of the order

If you were involved with the order in any way, it was really exciting. If you were ordering from a closed hospital, a nurse had to call the takeaway place and pay (with your money) instead of you. If we'd ordered too much, which often happened, we gave our spare food to a non-smoker, or some other person outside the main social group. Again, we knew the food was unhealthy, but we didn't see we had a choice. We ate fast food whenever we felt like it when I was in both the open and closed hospitals. Today, I've heard that, in some hospitals, patients are only allowed to order food on Wednesdays. I feel sorry for those patients. It's a great social event when the patients ordered food together. I guess someone must have ordered alcohol too many times and so the whole process was banned.

The multicultural nature of the staff

During my time staying in hospitals, it seems that every nationality was represented. There were Mongolians, Nigerians, Malaysians, Welsh, Mexican – every kind of person. I felt I could tell some of those nurses all my fears and nightmares. This would often be at times when I was extremely vulnerable. As far as I know, each of them respected my privacy once I'd bared my soul to them. I grew to respect all different nationalities and races more and more as time went on. I think all races are capable of friendship, and more than capable of hard work. I think to judge people based only on looks is lazy and stupid and people end up getting hurt in some way.

My smoking jacket

For a week or so, I was always to be found swanning about the hospital in a heavy, deep red dressing gown. I told everyone I met that it was my smoking jacket. I thought I was a member of a private gentleman's club, or something else posh like that. I even wore this gentleman's club gown into a ward round meeting. The doctor didn't extend my leave that week - a classic example of grandiose delusions!

Singing for cigarettes

Then, there was the time when everybody was nervous around one patient in particular. He always lit his cigarette with both elbows sticking out at shoulder-height. It was like he wanted to command as much personal space as possible while he did this. I asked him if he could lend me a cigarette, and he squared-up to me, ready for a fight. He was a bit taller than me, but I kept meeting his eye. So, while still looking at him, I burst into song. It caught him so off guard that he gave me a cigarette. Sometimes, social mores and doctrines can disappear out the window in those hospitals.

Kissing corpses

I grew extra paranoid about one patient in particular. I thought she was the Devil in human form. In a room full of people smoking, she'd soon be talking about religion. She was always telling everyone how she'd "kissed more dead bodies than you'd had hot dinners," at various funerals over the years. She'd always bring this up. She'd explain how cold and lifeless they were, and how, truth be told, she'd rather have seen them dead anyway. As far back as she could remember, she'd been made to kiss her elderly relatives and friends of the family as they lay there in their open coffin – dead, dressed-up and cold-to-the-touch.

She reigns in hell

I soon decided that this corpse-kissing woman was the Devil. I thought also that there were different realms in hell, some further down than others – I've never researched it for real. It was St Peter's job to decide whose soul goes up and who goes down after they die *during these times, my mind would be racing. I'd be thinking about the nurses there and why they're moving their feet like that; I wonder if those two are sleeping together; why doesn't that bloke look up – has there been a death in the family recently? I bet she got stoned last night; these people only work with the mentally ill to distract from their own illness; he wants a pay rise; she is really sexy, I wonder if she has a boyfriend, or girlfriend? – all kinds of stuff, but on the outside: "So, how are you feeling now?" "Fine, doctor. Thank-you." To be fair, he's paid to catch you out, so it's not always this easy to get distracted.* Once you were in heaven, you were safe and relaxed with God. Once you were in hell, the Devil was the commander of your soul. At the Devil's discretion, your soul would descend to whichever realm of hell he felt you deserved. Each of the different areas of hell was ruled by a different monster. At the time, I was sure I was going to hell and I was worried. I'd upset God, so I was going to hell. I'm sometimes a practical man and I figured that if God' had already excommunicated me, I might as well forget about heaven altogether. If I'm already going to hell, I might as well try to talk the Devil into getting a better deal. So, from that point on, I had to worship the Devil (so to speak) however this middle-aged mother-of-two felt about me.

Worshipping the Devil

For me to worship the Devil, I didn't need to draw a pentagram on the floor, with candles all around. I didn't need to get a group together under a church, torture a pure and innocent baby and get the rush from drinking its high-adrenaline blood (I've read about this somewhere since). I didn't need to make cuts in my body for hours on end and let them bleed out. I had the Devil right there with me in a very real way (which, for a Satanist, would be the blessing of a lifetime). So, I made her tea. And I made her toast. All the time. I was constantly at her beck and call, in fact. This woman must've wondered why I was being so kind, but why would she want it to stop? I was bringing her nice things all the time. Sometimes, I was bringing her things she hadn't even asked me to get. It was eerie, but I was sure my eternal soul would benefit from this pandering. I was certain of this lady's ability to judge the depths and durations of people's hellish punishments.

Damage control

So, I was hell bound *bizarrely, perhaps, an important factor here was that the decisions of these gods and monsters were already confirmed. It mattered not that you were on the verge of doing something insanely kind and positive. These plans didn't seem to matter. It was simply a matter of all your past achievements at this point which would go on to define your afterlife. I was effectively forced to be living always in the moment. I hated it.* My favours should surely take the edge off a bit, though? Maybe I'd be allowed to have a pleasant memory occasionally? Maybe I'd be given occasional breaks from being tortured now and then? I'd realised by this point that when I'd somehow insulted God, that'd sealed my fate – it was watertight. This was basically now urgent damage control for me. Either of these powerful deities could get transferred off the ward at any point. They'd be away from me and I'd never see them again. I didn't have long to sweet talk the Devil.

God and the Devil are friends now?

One day, during this rollercoaster, soul-destination politics, I saw who I thought were God and the Devil together in the same room through a window. They were both deep in conversation, standing in an otherwise empty smoking room. I already knew that the God character didn't smoke so that was strange. I could've sworn that they were simultaneously in the same hospital at the behest of the hospital manager. He'd granted the God-character special permission to be there for as long as they needed, which turned out to be for about ten minutes. Even though they were soundproofed in that room, everyone knew they were discussing me. What would they decide?

Deities plot against me

These two figures were supposed to be opposites with nothing in common. I thought they were working on ways to increase my suffering. I knew that no act of compassion or self-sacrifice would ever change this punishment. I'd been excommunicated by God and the Devil. I wasn't yet ready to tell any of the nurses (including those I'd confessed to before) about these worries. The Devil's reputation in society and media was overwhelming. Everybody seemed to be a default Satanist *any distancing from or denouncing God or Jesus, as far as some are concerned, constitutes Devil worship. Any contact with the dead – however reassuring or hope-inspiring - would be classed as necromancy. The person goes to hell. This results in most of the world being classed as an atheist, and by definition (not accepting Jesus as your saviour), a Satanist. At least, this is the way I saw it. I thought there were far more Satanists in the world than Christians – even if they were unaware that they were Satanists.* At the end of the day, who'd want to knowingly offend the Devil – her being a polite, generous mother-of-two? Or even God – him being a rude, shuffling, old man?

My Dad's descent into hell

At the time, I was powerless. Before long, my mind took a turn for the worse. I'd be idly thinking again about my family - how they'd be tortured because of me. I started wondering down to which depth of hell they'd be cast. My Dad soon came to mind. He'd been murdered by a Satanist because of me and now I was being shown his soul slowly descending. All the way as I watched him falling, he was saying to me in a quiet voice:

"You had so many times to do right, son. So many times."

Flesh-eating scorpions

I felt like someone had just ripped out my heart. I'd upset both the Devil and God – albeit unwittingly –and now my family were fair game. Once below the surface of the earth, my Dad was given back his earthly body, so he could feel physical pain again. He was then arranged upside-down with his face in a small crack at the bottom of a cave. In that cave were hundreds of flesh-eating scorpions. My Dad knew, as he was falling, that he had no need to shout his last audible words to me. He'd paved the way for my success whenever and wherever he could, trying to help me out. I'd never felt so much guilt and regret in my life - as I saw all these images in my mind's eye. Because of me, this man was now embarking on a new life in hell. I could see all this whenever I closed my eyes.

My brother's descent into hell

My brother went to somewhere else in hell. Where he fell to, he was to be raped by a wooden monster in a large, perpetually-twilit forest-clearing. There were a few bushes dotted about where he could hide for a bit. Then, the monster would yell and the bushes would move. After a while, he started sending me messages like my Dad had - of how close we could have been if I hadn't messed up my life by constantly getting stoned. Obviously, most of his energy was devoted to escaping the pain he faced. At the times when there was a brief respite for him, it was because the monster had zeroed-in on another poor soul down there instead. It was during these times that my brother would send me his hopeless messages. After that, he'd hide behind a bush and the cat-and-mouse game would start all over again. The guilt and regret I felt, as I saw him down there in pain, almost engulfed me entirely. Again, because I couldn't see my brother for real at the time, or talk to him, all of this seemed like it could have been possible.

Gypsy bloodbath

One day, I was talking to another patient about a bad childhood memory he had. He was from a Romany gypsy family living in a tower block a few miles away. About twenty-five years before, he'd witnessed up close a massive, bloody gang-fight. At the time, he was only about five. A simple argument had quickly turned into carnage. People in both families (of all ages and both sexes) were using all sorts of different weapons (knives, hammers, swords) with which to attack one another. Dan saw all this happen, and the horror of that night had stayed with him ever since. He was still having the same nightmares now, at the age of thirty. They drove him to distraction to such a degree that he ultimately took his own life.

The dangerous man

Another time, there was a stocky Irish man who'd tell people, even at the smallest slight:

"I'm a dangerous man". No arguing.

He definitely looked dangerous. I'm quite a happy-go-lucky bloke, though, so soon, I was teaching him to make roll-ups. It started out with me just making them for him. My fee was one roll-up for every three I'd make for him – using his tobacco. I didn't mind that, it gave me something to do and saved me from using my own stuff. The way he put it, he wasn't used to living on the breadline, he was used to luxury. Most of the other patients in the hospital feared him, partly because he'd told them to.

Family dispute leads to jail time

Another man I met (Joe) had been sent to prison after a big fight with his Dad. Joe had smashed one of the windows in his Dad's house. His Dad then called the police and had Joe arrested. Joe couldn't read and write, so I read his legal letters to him. There were never enough nurses on duty to do this, so I felt I had to. He offered me some advice if I was ever thrown in prison. Even if all the other prisoners were in the yard mixing together, I should remain in my cell. This was because while you were out, the Guards or other prisoners could go in your cell and take your stuff. If they really didn't like you, they could plant drugs, weapons or phones in your room, and then report you to the guards.

Rumours of the hospital gym

You couldn't really exercise in the hospital. You could sign up to go to the gym, but that took ages. To get signed up, all the nurses had a meeting and, after a few weeks, you could train then. Usually, when you were finally allowed, the motivation you originally had would've dissipated. Nine times out of ten, they'd call for you in the morning. Of course, the morning is a time when no-one wants to do anything, let alone lift weights or jog for half an hour. At that time of day, even the most eager patient would usually rather just go back to sleep. The hospital gym was an incredible place, if you believed some people. Rumour had it, there were rows and rows of treadmills, lots of Rotex machines, free-weights and other weights machines. There was also a full-sized punch-bag and lots of mats on which you could stretch. At about ten in the morning (once a week), the lucky few patients were collected and taken there. After what seemed like months, I qualified enough to go with them.

The gym show-off

There was no way the place could live up to its reputation. One man would always get back from his gym time with a small towel still draped over his shoulders. He'd make sure everyone noticed the towel, and then tell everyone where he'd just been. He'd also tell everyone how many sets and reps he'd just done. Once, he'd told us how they'd run out of extra plates to add to the ends of his barbell, because he could lift so much. Other people I spoke to had said the gym was small, dusty and covered in cobwebs. My inaugural gym visit happened one Tuesday. The place turned out to be quite small, but the equipment they had was decent enough. There was one of each of the machines/ stations there. My favourite, initially, was the punch bag. That first time, it was a female nurse who took me there. She held the punch bag for me while I threw all sorts of punches and kicks at it. She was a bit smaller than me, but she knew what to do: gamely taking the bag and shouldering it like a trainer would. After a first few jabs, I got going. During those first few minutes, I unleashed weeks and weeks of pent-up anger onto that bag. By the time I'd finished, I was really sweating. The nurse with me was laughing her head off. I started laughing, too. I'd put some real ferocity into some of those moves, even doing the noises I'd heard boxers do with their noses. Of course, while I was going at it, she was doing her best to hold on. It was a great introduction to the gym.

My first workout

When I went with the patient with the towel to the gym, he spent the whole time warming-up and chatting with the nurse – I didn't see him lift a single weight. He was still wearing his jeans and he wasn't even warming-up properly. He was doing his warm-ups so badly they couldn't really have counted as stretches. As for me, I always made good use of my time there. It may have been a bit geeky, but I knew what I was doing. I'd waited for weeks to start trying to get back in shape. Whenever I went, I always made sure I was dressed correctly: loose T-shirt, jogging bottoms and trainers. I also had a house music mix (via my minidisc player) in my earphones, a towel for sweat and a small bottle of water. A big part of me knew I was pissing in the wind really. It was going to be impossible trying to lose weight while I was still in the hospital every day doing nothing. After my workout, I knew I'd just go back to the ward and laze around again. I'd go back to stuffing my face with toast, jam, Weetabix and full-fat milk. I'd start chain-smoking again from where I'd left off. It really wasn't worth the hassle of exercising, really. So, after a few weeks gamely attempting to get fitter, I gave up trying and stopped going.

Walking around the grounds

Another chance to get a bit fitter was to walk around the grounds. If you had no leave to the grounds at this point, it was even more special. A nurse would round up a group of patients, and we'd go down some off-the-ward stairs to begin. Only people with a greenlight from the doctor were allowed on these walks. We quickly did some proper stretches and we were good to go. The route was a huge lap all around the hospital grounds' perimeter. At a fast pace, it could be really tiring. Usually, the nurse doing it would keep us all motivated. A group of layabout smokers like us needed a lot of help to stay focussed. Exercise Sessions fell under the umbrella of the OT (Occupational Therapy) department. If you took part in any OT sessions, your doctor was always informed of how it went at ward round. Any positive participation with OT would help you achieve more leave in the long term.

Massage

Another OT activity was massage. The masseuse always brought her own collapsible, massage table along with her in a travel case with little wheels. Along with the table, she also had a small boom box and some essential oils. She'd massage your hands, arms and neck – unless you had a pain somewhere else. When the time was up, you booked in to see her again the following week.

The posh art therapist

Art therapy, another OT class, was not for me. Patients with children on the outside would delight in making personalised arts and crafts for them. They'd usually make cards using glitter and paint. The messages would be things like:

"Mummy loves you loads", or:

"When Daddy's out again, we'll all go to the zoo".

With no children of my own, these art sessions would drag on and on. I was only there so the doctors would increase my leave at ward round. So, in one of these art classes, I was angrier than usual. On top of this, the man taking the class was ridiculously posh, with a really condescending voice. Every time he opened his mouth all I could hear was:

"I'm so rich and posh that I don't have to do anything for work. I'm still richer than you and everyone you know put together because I'm so great and much better than you at everything – la di dah. I'm only taking this class so I can trash you all to my super-wealthy friends afterwards. My family own most of Yorkshire, don't y' know? I'm inheriting a moat tomorrow – an infinity moat. Where's the nearest airstrip? Where's the concierge? How do you get room service? I'm surrounded by peasants!" So, I grabbed my chance to get even.

Red paint

I'd never seen the man before, he must've been new. As soon as the class started, I got hold of some blank card, white paper and a brand-new tube of red paint. I took the top off the paint, broke the seal, and sat there staring at my assorted items.

"And what would you like to do today, then?"

It was none of his business! I was furious. I looked at him and looked back down at my papers. Then, I took the tube of paint in both hands and squeezed the whole thing onto the things in front of me. It made a huge, wet mess. I forget how he initially reacted. I was still gripping the empty paint tube as tightly as I could, getting all the last little bits out. After I'd used up all the red paint, I put the other pieces of card and paper into the puddle and slid them all amongst one another. The whole time, I was careful not to impinge upon anyone else's work. This was just the therapy I needed. I had to vent my anger and I felt great after I'd used up all the red paint (I knew there was more on the other table). I was banned from art therapy, after that, but I'd made my point.

Gardening therapy

Also available to patients was OT gardening. This was also weekly, but could be called off if the weather was bad. I couldn't see the point in getting muddy and tired when you could sit in the warm and smoke. Most people did gardening to impress the doctors, but for me, it wasn't even worth that. Their garden kept winning local prizes, so at least the OT nurses knew what they were doing.

Cookery

Right next to the garden was the main OT suite – complete with kitchen. This was the venue for cookery. Nurses would assemble all the relevant patients and give us all a meal to cook. Then, we'd cook and eat that meal. After a few months of this, they let us decide which meal we cooked. There'd be an extra session where the nurses took everyone to the supermarket to get the ingredients for the meal. If the weather was ok, these little shopping trips could be great fun.

Palindrome phrases

I thought that when people spoke, they were conscious of the number of letters there were in the words and phrases they used. The phrases could mean the same thing, but they'd either be respectful or disrespectful.

An example of a respectful way of putting something would be:

"Be upstanding," where the longest word comes at the end.

A disrespectful phrase would be:

"Stand up," where the longest word comes at the beginning.

Phrases like "every little helps" or "terrible business" wouldn't be disrespectful or respectful, because the number of letters in each of the words used is identical - like a macro-palindrome.

Why phrase it like that?

These are quite difficult to create, according to the rules. When I first started worrying about this, it plagued my mind for ages. Was the nurse serving food being consciously disrespectful about the greens? Should I avoid them, or ask for more?

"Delicious sprouts here!"

Or was this nurse (the next day) being respectful on purpose?

"D' you want some cabbage?"

I was in knots trying to figure out who was enemy or who was ally. Ward rounds during this period were overwhelmingly confusing. I'd be sitting there thinking I was the only person who couldn't keep up with the numbers of letters in phrases, while actually, no-one cared and they were talking on a usual level of understanding. One nurse might refer to my condition as "grandiose delusions;" another as "delusions of grandeur". I was more relaxed speaking to the nurse who used the first phrase, since it was one of those rare macro-palindrome phrases.

Demon adds "yet"

This balancing of word lengths was constantly happening mentally also. I'd count the letters of something I'd just *thought* and rephrase/rethink it quickly if it could be improved. I was just getting used to this when I was rudely interrupted. I'd think something like "I love this hospital" and a demon would add "...yet" after I'd finished. "I want to sleep tremendously" – "yet." Or: "I'm feeling peaceful," - "...yet". Since the last word was always small, the balance of the entire phrase was altered. I could never have the safe thoughts I wanted to have. It was forcing me to be disrespectful. I hated that thing.

Creative writing therapy

In the name of getting discharged faster, I went to OT's creative-writing group. The classes were boring, though. I was writing lots of my own poetry as it was, and I wasn't ready to write more. I put my poems everywhere. I displayed poetry on the wall by the canteen, on the walls of the hospital and the walls of the lift, everywhere – all with nurses' permission. One time, I put a poem up right next to someone else's. Then, the first poem vanished. The lady who'd written it must have read mine, compared them, then removed her poem. When I realised what she'd done, I was chuffed. Then, after my triumphant surge, I pitied her a bit.

Jailbreak

Then, it dawned on me how I could rescue everyone in the hospital and set them all free. Lots of different bus routes terminated not far from the entrance to the hospital. I thought we could swarm one of the bus drivers and take his bus. First, we had to tie up all the nurses in the hospital. The thing about worried and depressed patients is that they're usually deep in thought about something – not that most could explain what was on their minds. The nurses often must rely on this phenomenon. If one patient flips out, it can take the entire team of nurses to calm him/her down. When this happens, the other patients are unsupervised for a little while. I wanted all twenty male and female patients to simultaneously lose their tempers, and then rush the nurses. Sadly, for me and my plan, no-one really knows when or where a psychotic person will get angry – one reason why the disease is so misunderstood. One big flaw in my plan was that everyone was on tranquilisers. Also, a psychotic person usually isn't thinking about the future at all, let alone taking part in a co-ordinated escape plan requiring teamwork. During a psychotic episode, a patient of either sex can have the strength of ten people, but these episodes can be impossible to predict. The word we used was to "switch". It was like a switch had been thrown in the patient's mind. They would instantly go from calm to angry.

Collecting passports

So, we'd all switch at the same time and storm the nurses. We'd seize the keys, go through the heavy doors, go downstairs and then we'd be outside. In the carpark, we'd storm the bus driver, tie him up and take his bus. We'd drive to people's houses and collect their passports. Then, we'd head to France. Once we'd crossed the channel, we'd share the driving and go to Russia, India or China. As I discussed the plan there in the smoking room alone to one of the patient's capos, the plan was flawless.

Dangerous people

You can often hear this kind of escape talk when people are locked-up and grouped together. I always found it interesting how much manpower the police set aside for catching mental patients who'd run off. Most of the ones I've known were calm people for the most part. The golden rules the doctors tell you are:

- Don't be a danger to yourself; and
- Don't be a danger to others.

So really, if you keep your wits about you and you're careful, you should be fine.

Bad telephone manner

Sometimes, I'd walk around blaring loud gangster rap music. I'd have my phone playing in my jeans pocket with the volume all the way up. I must've seemed quite threatening to some of the older patients. I basically didn't give a shit. It's fair to say I was psychotic at the time, which can't have helped. Music-wise, things don't get more violent. The flow of the rhyming was peppered with swearing, screaming and gunshots. I think I got away with it for the most part because one of my friends liked what I was doing. He was a lot scarier than me, which was probably why people left me alone. One time, I was fuming for some reason when the patients' phone rang. Still furious, I went up to the ringing phone. I lifted it to my face and yelled:

"Fuck off! Everyone's dead!"

Then, I slammed down the phone as hard as I could and stomped off somewhere else.

Mafia recruitment schools

I thought that mental hospitals throughout the world were funded largely by the Mafia. The patients were all being slowly and surreptitiously trained to kill people for them. They were exploiting the concept of "diminished responsibility". The idea was that a patient would first get discharged. Then, they'd meet a friendly nurse (covert Mafia) out and about. They'd then be talked into killing someone for the Mafia. The patient/ killer would plead insanity in the courtroom and get off with a much lesser sentence. Years before this unsubstantiated theory, I'd thought something similar in central London. I thought young people were being given jobs as hit men and women because they could aim well playing shoot-'em-ups in selected amusement arcades. They'd be discovered playing Time Crisis, Sniper's Scope or some other first-person shoot-'em-up videogame. Clearly, I'd been watching too many gangster movies, but at the time, I really believed it.

Up late with the scavenger

One night, I was up smoking after evening meds (at 10pm) with another man. He was a scavenger. Normally, he'd be begging everyone for the tiniest piece of tobacco – even no visitor was safe. Then, he'd set about trying to find dirty, little dog-ends from the ashtrays. He'd break the dog-ends apart and smoke the old tobacco from those. He could've been doing it as a guilt trip for the rest of us, but that may have just been a side-effect of his constant searching. Still, the ashtrays there were shallow and perfect for people like him. One of the other patients grew to hate this scavenger man so much that he'd empty these shallow ashtrays into the long, tube-shaped bin underneath. This would effectively put any extra tobacco completely out of range for the scavenger. I thought this was maybe a bit cruel, but I could understand his motives.

Ten cups of tea and coffee

So, on this night, the scrounger was smoking his own tobacco, which took the pressure off me. We all knew the pantry was locked at midnight so this man was making hay while the sun shone. With moments to spare, he'd made about ten cups of tea and coffee. I could see him lining them all up on the kitchen counter, all piping hot and sugared the way he liked. He added milk to each, and started bringing them all slowly into the smoking room. He'd begun his drinks-making with about fifteen minutes to go, when the pantry was locked for the night. He'd timed it perfectly. He knew that after a nurse locks the pantry door, the only drinks available were lemon and orange cordial. He must've thought he was beating the system. He was easily in his late fifties but he was carrying on like a teenager.

My theory on comfort food

During the night, you could ask a nurse to go to the vending machines for you, which were just outside the first two heavy doors. £1 bought you a 500ml bottle of Coke and 50p would get you a packet of crisps. They usually had Nic-Nacs or beef McCoys. If my luck was in, there'd be salt and vinegar McCoys there. With all the worry and sadness around, food was a brilliant, cheap form of comfort. The waistline could wait. What I think is that when you're eating food, you're owning it, in a way. If you don't feel in charge of other things in your life, at least you had food. Just putting something in your mouth to crunch, chew and swallow made you the physical master of something – you'd consumed it, physically engulfed it. I think therefore comfort eaters get a little thrill during and after eating something they shouldn't? Also, if the food is junk food, there's the forbidden fruit factor, as well. This means they feel twice as good. Obviously, they won't feel that great when they break out the scales and none of their clothes fit them anymore.

Uncomfortable silence

So, I watched this patient finally finish bringing all his hot drinks into the smoking room. The nurse duly locked the pantry behind him. This man made the coffee table his own, putting all his drinks on that. There was only me in there with him. He seemed happy in silence and strangely even put the lights low. The TV had just been turned off, so he split his focus between his group of hot drinks and smoking his own cigarettes. Rumours were circulating that this man had been accused of child abuse in the 60s. I hate to say it, but he did seem creepy to me. I always remember how he used to refer to the dozens of fruit cordials he had stored in his room as his "fluids".

Naturally annoying

Over the years, he'd sometimes be allocated the bedroom next to mine. He always played his radio too loud. He listened to a different station every night – he called it "connecting with his people". It'd be late at night and the whole rest of the hospital's asleep and, naturally, I'd be trying to sleep, too. On more than one occasion, he'd fall asleep with the radio and the main light on. When this happened, I'd have to fetch a member of staff to unlock the man's door, then turn off the radio and then turn off the light. Somehow, he managed to sleep through all of this. It was a relief for him not to be pestering me for cigarettes or anything else. He'd also be forever shouting about how much he loved his wife. The two of them had suffered on and off with mental illness for decades. I'd known both (only in hospital) for years. Because they were married, they had to be kept in different parts of the hospital. Canoodling (kissing or tender touching between patients) was always a danger.

The married couple

These two belligerent people always found a way to communicate. If they weren't on the phone to each other, they'd yell back and forth. You'd hear the husband shouting:

"I love you, and I always will! You still love me, don't you?"

He'd shout all this as loud as he could through the windows facing his wife's room. She didn't always answer. So, he'd repeat his statement at a higher volume. If she did shout back, it was something like:

"Shut up, you silly bastard! Of course I do!"

I found it all a bit desperate, but that's how it was.

Planting cocaine

I really had a lot on my mind. I was sure beyond doubt that I was soon about to be arrested. I was to be charged with supplying cocaine – not that I'd had any actual contact with cocaine. I knew that supplying a class A drug often came with a heavy prison sentence. I thought my Mum and my brother (of all people) had hidden some cocaine in my flat. They'd hidden a kilo or so of the stuff in my flat, somewhere I'd never find it.

Itchy face giveaway

As if to encourage my paranoia, my face started to really get itchy. I thought an itchy face was proof you were a drug addict – much like driving with an open nearside window can indicate drink-driving. If the nurses saw me scratching, especially around my nose, I thought the staff would have me immediately arrested by the police – it was inevitable. I didn't want to go to prison. So, I'd walk around the hospital with my face covered with annoying, little itches – although there was never any evidence of a rash. I had to just leave them unscratched because I couldn't risk people seeing me scratching my face and nose. If you've ever felt an itch that would take a big body movement, then just let it itch and itch – you'll find that (if nothing's actually stinging you), it'll stop itching with no further action. After a while, I figured I could always go somewhere private and scratch all the annoying, facial itches. But I was still really worried about the police arriving.

Superstitious button fly

I thought my brother had gone in my flat and left a bag of unusually pure cocaine somewhere inside. He'd hidden it somewhere I'd never find it. I'd go back to my flat while on leave. He'd anonymously call the police and tell them I was a big dealer of cocaine. I was in a tailspin of powerful paranoia. If I even buttoned-up the flies on my jeans in the wrong way, there was cause for panic. Of the five buttons, I had to be careful to only do up the ones I was being told (in my head) to do. If I got it wrong, I'd rush back to the bathroom and do them up differently.

X-ray vision for drugs

After a while, the itching problem subsided. Now I had a bigger problem. I was panicking about my X-ray vision. I could just about make out various criminals committing crimes throughout the night. I understood that amounts of cash and amounts of weapons went together with amounts of cocaine and other class A drugs. If the police found two, they'd usually find the third there, too. I'd see peoples' homes with their cocaine shipments glowing yellow in my mind's eye. Guns and explosives glowed a dark purple colour. I couldn't see cash with my X-ray vision.

Thoughts monitored by the nurses

I knew my thoughts were being watched by the nurses. I knew that vocalising these worries was impossible – I'd be fobbed off with some poor excuse. They had my body in the hospital under lock and key, and now they wanted my thoughts as well. I thought that, by law, the nurses had to pass on to the police everything they'd found psychically through me. This meant lots of raids being carried out that night - in real time, in real neighbourhoods – with me floating around gathering damning evidence for the police, against my will. Major weapons and drugs stashes all over London were (sometimes simultaneously) getting seized by police. What's more, the criminals knew (on a very low vibration) that it was me. The criminals and their friends knew exactly where to find me. At this point, I was afraid and, because I thought my family were in with the criminals now too, very alone.

I watch the raids and arrests

So, I watched as people were attacked and shot by police; and police were being shot, too. It felt like I was watching a film. I could see the yellow-glowing cocaine, the purple-glowing weapons and doors getting smashed in as police raided the houses. There was a lot of yelling and handcuffing people. I'd caused all the raids and the criminals knew that. Because of me, cartels within about 100 miles of my location were getting disrupted. I couldn't control the madness and badly wanted it to stop.

When the whole wing wants you dead

So, at that time, I was really worried about all the drug dealers' friends coming for me. On top of that, there were the police officers who'd been tipped-off that I myself was dealing. Their arresting me would be the first domino in a line that would result in my being thrown in jail for many years. It had reached the point where I'd been put in touch (solely through paranoid telepathy) with the prisoner with whom I was going to share a cell. As soon we made contact, he emphasised that I was hated in prison already. I was so nervous that for weeks, I couldn't even do my own washing. My socks smelled terrible *during these weeks, I could barely leave my room. I trusted no-one. Using the hospital washing machine meant leaving your clothes to wash for about an hour. Every time I thought I could leave my clothes, there'd appear another patient. I had no allies in there at that time. Someone was known to be stealing clothes on the ward, and if I stayed to watch my clothes safely wash (then dry in the dryer, which took nearly as long) I knew I'd be accused as the thief. Bearing all this in mind, I thought I'd just leave my clothes as they were. I tried washing some of my clothes with a bar of soap, but quickly gave up. The stench could be almost overwhelming. I was constantly arguing with the staff about it.* I could smell them while I had them on my feet, as I lay flat on my back in my bed. Soon, word spread around my future prison that I had smelly socks. This shortcoming was a fast-track to endless beatings and humiliation. The whole wing was now baying for my blood. My only healthy step forward was to grit my teeth and throw myself on a nurse's mercy.

I confess my cocaine paranoia

I chose my confessor carefully. These cocaine thoughts had tangled me up for weeks. I had to tell somebody or I'd just explode. A growing part of me had started thinking it was all fantasy. It was these doubts that propelled me forward. I thought I risked death threats and smashed windows. If I'd really disrupted multinational drug cartels, they'd already be coming after me anyway. I had nothing to lose.

One-to-ones

I went up to a trusted nurse and set up a "one-to-one" as they were known. I detailed all my fears to him while, initially at least, every night it continued. Even just talking about your concerns to someone can be enough for them to start receding. If I was thinking any dark thoughts, the one-to-one would expose them to the light. Then, the worries would leave or at least morph into something else. Chasing them about my head like this was much better than following one kind of nightmare down and down without any coming up for air.

Shot at by a nurse

Out of nowhere, a group of men like zombies with massive sharp teeth pounced on me and surrounded me and started tearing me apart. Then I remembered there was a trusted nurse just outside the door. I turned my thoughts to him for help. When I did this, he appeared to me and started shooting at me through the wall! I then tried to stop thinking about him, but he stayed angry. After I'd mustered up the courage, I left my bedroom (physically, this time) and approached him:

(Addressing my recent hallucination) "Why did you shoot at me just now? What have I done wrong?"

Obviously, he looked blank and denied having shot me. But if he hated me so much, he would deny it! They say that schizophrenics can't always distinguish between fact and fantasy. All I know is that it took quite a while for me to trust that nurse again.

The bulimic girl

There was a girl with bulimia in there with me. You could see it in her teeth, where so many times puking had begun melting them away. She told me she could "feel the fat and sugar sticking to her thighs" if she didn't get to privacy and puke ASAP after eating. She was already thin, but still wanted to get thinner. She'd often refuse to eat and would even keep fit by dancing in her room. Every dinner time, the nurses would make her eat something. She'd yell and scream and run off. I was discharged ahead of her, while she remained there. I was out for about eighteen months, then I smoked another joint, became ill, and was readmitted. The girl with bulimia was still in the hospital, but her bulimia seemed to have gone. Now, she loved her main courses and always asked for seconds and sometimes thirds. Following that, she'd want extra chocolate sauce or custard on her pudding.

Sharing a bedroom

There have been a few times when I've had to share a room. A double room was only really a problem if the other person snored. At one point, to keep the peace, the nurses gave me extra meds to help me sleep. With a snorer, it was a whole night of guiltily waking him up, which stops the snoring, only to tell him to stop snoring. Then, he falls back asleep again and the snoring begins afresh. One man I was sharing with was trying to sleep, but kept fidgeting. I thought he'd maybe had too much coffee. Still, he was always kicking out his feet and I could hear him rustling his sheets all the time. Since then, I've learned that all the kicking is something heroin addicts do when they're trying to come off the drug. They call it "kicking the habit" because of all the twitching the rehabbing addict does with his legs. A single room was like heaven compared to this.

The verbose man

There was one elderly man in the hospital who I'd met/ shared a ward with a few times. He was incessantly talking under his breath about other patients who were "drug barons". He'd ramble on about how he'd report them to Scotland Yard. Either it was that, or how all the nurses were paid-up members of the Nazi party or how he himself was of royal blood. If you tried to talk to him normally, he'd just look the other way and keep on babbling. It was as if what he was saying didn't really matter, just as long as he was saying *something*.

My coping strategy

Sometimes, if this man was feeling extra testy, he'd try and start a fight (he had a slight build with a distant look to him). His favourite chair was along one wall of the main corridor. When he was feeling combative, he'd look for trouble with anybody who walked along the busy corridor and past his chair. Although he never raised his voice, he'd start swearing and repeat his insults if he felt they were inflammatory enough. I developed a method of coping with people like him. As I walked past, I'd repeat the word "nothing" over and over to myself in my head until his vitriol was out of earshot again. Dismissing his unfocussed, yet quiet, aggression like this always worked, deflating any tension there might have been.

The Moroccan

For a short while, there was a patient there who'd landed in the UK from Morocco. He'd come into the country somehow, and now he was mentally ill. I think just being in this country can make some people ill. Immigrants come here to the UK to seek their fortune and it all goes wrong. I'd seen this happen with my African friend, also. Maybe England is just a tense place for some people? We didn't really say much to each other, me and the Moroccan, but what we did say was brilliant. We were always insulting one another. I think the style of the insults is normal in the Middle East. It was all quite light-hearted and funny. Usually, the insults involved family members and animals.

Scathing family insults

For example, I'd be minding my own business, in the smoking-room smoking. Then, he'd come in and say:

"Your mother is a goat and your father is the son of a camel".

Then I'd say:

"Your sister is a baboon's whore. And when she walks by, people collapse because she smells so bad".

Then he'd say:

"Your brother gives old men blow jobs to pay for crack".

I'd say:

"Your grandmother is the cross-dressing son of a donkey".

We didn't talk that much

Anyone who heard us talking would think we hated each other, the way we laid into one another like that. Afterwards, we always fell about laughing. It was great fun. Oddly, apart from the insults, we didn't talk that much. The more I think about it, I'm not even sure our talks were out loud - I think all the funny insults were in my head. It was such a long time ago. He had the habit of grinning broadly at you when he looked at you. This made you feel like he could understand your thoughts. The more I think about it, I think we just never spoke.

Setting off the fire alarm

About once a month, the female patients would purposely set off the fire alarm. Every few weeks, they'd burn some toast in the pantry and the fire alarm would sound. Those women knew that the fire station was automatically notified when this happened. So, within about half an hour, there'd be a group of battle-ready firefighter son the ward. While the firemen were around, it seemed like all the women became giggling teenagers. They'd discuss the firefighters' long hoses, big helmets, that sort of thing. Once the firefighters had sealed off the pantry and surmised that burnt toast had set off the alarm, they'd explain to the culprit the dangers of crying wolf and they'd leave. Probably, in the back of their mind, they suspected it was going to be a matter of toast, but they couldn't take the risk. One woman set fire to the curtains in her room a few times, but she wasn't doing it to summon firefighters. The nurses confiscated her lighter, but we all gave her a light in the smoking room anyway.

Personal information

One time, I'd been moved for canoodling. I found myself sitting next to a gorgeous girl from somewhere in Eastern Europe. Her name was Natasha and she didn't speak much English. Everything she said sounded sexy. Because her English was broken, she had a catch-all phrase ready for when people got too close.

Me: "How are you?"

Natasha: "Fine."

Me: "Could I ask you some questions?"

Natasha: "If you like."

Me: "Where are you from?"

Natasha: "That is personal information."

Me: "Have you been sectioned?"

Natasha: "That is personal information."

Me: "Have you eaten?"

Natasha: "That is personal information."

...So sexy.

Canoodlers

Then, she came closer and seductively draped herself all over me. There was another man in the smoking room with us at the time. He probably thought I was gay, because I didn't respond to any of the passes she made at me. The way I saw it, I'd already been caught canoodling once, and moved off my original ward because of it. If I got expelled again, would I be moved to a hospital hundreds of miles away? Also, gentleman that I am, part of me was trying to stay loyal to my original canoodler, who was still just a stone's throw away. It couldn't be anything good if you were caught canoodling twice. So, I somehow managed to ignore Natasha's sex kitten attempts at seducing me. All the while, she kept purring to me that everything was "personal information". Underneath it all, I felt like James Bond. It would've been easy for a lesser man to respond sexually, but I remained true. The more likely reason was that I didn't want my original canoodler to find out. She'd already broke protocol and pounced on me in bed once already, and that was when we were friends!

England's smoking ban

July 2007 was a terrible month for smokers in England. There was to be no more smoking indoors in public places, this also covered the hospital. Smokers had to smoke somewhere else. I'm a non-smoker now and I'm glad I stopped. At the time, it was crap. Of course, people get used to changes and we were no different. Sometimes, we would still secretly smoke in our rooms (as we always had), but for the official cigarettes, we had a brand-new place. It was called the "smoking pod" or "the pod" for short.

The pod

Each part of the hospital (and similar hospitals like it elsewhere in England) had a pod constructed and stuck on the side of it. It was like a small, add-on room. A pod was like a lift that didn't go anywhere. You'd go through the door and stand there with all the waist-high ashtrays and smoke. Because there were only metal bars from your waist down, the smoke would get blown away at waist height. From the waist up, there was toughened glass. If there were a lot of people out smoking at the same time, you could feel the pod moving slightly. And during the winter, it got very cold.

Cat and mouse with the chair

Often, we'd grab a chair from inside and bring it out, even though the nurses frowned upon chairs on the pod. Sometimes, one of the older patients would moan about having a bad back and then the chair was allowed. Otherwise, it was a matter of smuggling one there. The pod was open to us 24/7, except for a tense half hour every morning when it was cleaned. We were always desperate to smoke and some people would get angry with the cleaners in the morning.

Our version of Hell's Kitchen

After they added smoking pods to the hospital, things changed again a few months after that. Initially, you could yell at a friend in the other pod and he could yell back. The nurses brought an end to this, though, because there was too much shouting. So, they painted the pods' windows white. This did quiet things down a lot. Before they were painted, it felt like Hell's Kitchen in New York, from all the movies. Luke was always cheeky to the nurses. He was a real livewire and was well-respected. He used to yell at me, then ask me the same questions:

Luke: "Lend us a fiver!"

Me: "No,"

Luke: "A tenner?"

Me: "No,"

Luke: "A twenty?"

Me: "No,"

Luke: "Stay lucky!"

Me: "I will!"

To a stranger, it could seem a bit boisterous, but it was all in good humour. It was a fun way to pass the time.

Whistling messages

I also had a thing going with a girl on the other ward. We'd wave to each other first, then I'd whistle some random melody. All the while, I was watching her and really concentrating on what I wanted to say. She'd receive my message, understand what I was saying, and whistle something in reply. All a bystander would hear was our erratic, question-and-answer warbling, but we could communicate. Obviously, the hospital wasn't ideal for serious scientific experiments. If we'd put our whistling theories through clinical trials, they'd have almost certainly proven our thinking and whistling had no real substance.

Inhaling with different colours

I used to be concerned about inhaling cigarette smoke while holding another person's gaze. It'd be an insult to that person if I did. This also applied if I was watching TV and the person onscreen was looking out at me. Soon after the worries about this began, things got worse. I thought that coloured lasers from my eyes meant different things to the person. If I was inhaling and looking at a man, I had to think green. If I was looking at a woman and inhaling, it had to be pink. I had to look at them and think of these colours while holding their gaze. Seems crazy now, but to follow these rules at the time was crucial. Conversely, if I was inhaling the smoke from a joint while meeting someone's eye, it was good - no matter the colour I was thinking. Joints were somehow exempt.

Angry monologues

There was one man who'd often come barrelling into the smoking pod and come out with this kind of a speech:

"Yeah? Nah, mate. I ain't seen him. What? Nah… You fuckin' what?! You realise who I am? You're havin' a fuckin' bubble, mate! Tidy… Say what you just said again, I'll put you through the fuckin' wall! You're a c**t, mate! Yeah, mate! Yeah?! I'll 'ave fifteen of 'em. …Tuesday. You can fuck off an' all! Who? Wednesday, then! See ya later, mate! C**t..." Then - the thing that always grabbed me - he'd stay right where he was. After a short period of silence, he'd repeat the whole thing again from the start. The first time I'd heard him do his talk, I was alone with him and I was just about to reply. Then, when he ignored me, I thought he might be on the phone. After a while, I just accepted that this was the manifestation of his illness. Even when he had visitors, he was like that. The words were always a bit different, but the urgency was always there.

Unboxing a fresh pack of cigarettes

I used to love opening a new pack of cigarettes to get to the first one – especially if you were gasping. First, you took the plastic, red tearing strip. You pulled this off and the whole outer plastic film came away from around the box. Then, you lifted the little cardboard flap at the top of the box. Under this flap was some silver paper. You then pulled out the silver paper to reveal twenty small, white circles - the tips of all the cigarettes. Each little circle snug and willing to please. Then, you pulled one out and put it in your mouth ready to smoke. You sparked up your lighter, put the flame to the end of it and you were off. That first in-breath of cigarette smoke (the suffocation) could be almost euphoric. It was like you'd just got back in touch with a dear, old friend. That friend was always bad news, though. These days, I don't miss smoking. I much prefer having the extra money and more energy.

Smoke then gulp

I had a vocals coach for a while. He was asthmatic and

hated that I smoked. Because of this, I ensured I had a gulp of a tea, coffee, Diet Coke straight after a lungful of smoke. It was my concession to him because I wanted to protect my voice from drying out. I can still sing OK, so maybe it worked. 5th of October 2010 is the day I finally quit.

Gulping out of respect

I had the strange habit of "showing respect" to the room into which I was about to go. I needed a drink (such as a coffee or a hot chocolate) to do this, but I usually had one with me anyway. It was more like a show of respect for the people *in* that room, even if I didn't know who was in there, or sometimes if it was empty. I'd take a sip of my drink and make sure I swallowed the whole mouthful. Once I'd finished swallowing, I'd move reverentially through the door and into the room. I think I thought I was approaching it the way they would in Japan. All I really knew about the Japanese was that they had small pictures instead of words, they took drinking tea very seriously and they sometimes had paper walls between rooms. Also, they'd invented loads of martial arts (such as jujitsu and karate) and their Mafia members usually had full body tattoos hidden under their business suits. I never found out if they bothered finishing swallowing a mouthful of drink before they went into a new room. Still, I thought I was party to a secret Japanese custom no other Westerner knew.

My Superman avatar

One of my nightmares featured me as Superman. As Superman *I later discovered I had more in common with Superman than I'd thought. Kryptonite is a green*

substance, and it's Superman's only known weakness.
Skunk is a green substance which is my main weakness. I
thought this in passing once, then forgot about it. If I'd
avoided weed as strenuously as Superman avoids
Kryptonite, I could've drawn a line under the whole sorry
affair and moved on with my life far earlier, I'd orbit the
world looking down over it. Things were great, until my
actions were hijacked by an invisible demon. I tried to
resist it at first, but the demon was too strong. I flew
over the beaches of southern Australia. I could see all
the swimmers and the surfers having fun. Now, they
could all see Superman. And I was strong-armed into
elevating the entire landmass of Australia – from a grip
on its shoreline *I was doing it just like I'd seen*
Superman do it in the early films. In one of them, some
people were stuck in a fire. Superman found a lake
nearby and froze it with his icy cold breath. Then, he
lifted the big, lake-size lump of ice up out of the ground.
He carried the ice over to the blaze and dropped it onto
the fire. The people got out and were all really happy. I
lifted the country up into the air and then out into space.
Billions of gallons of seawater surrounding Australia
then spilled into the fresh cavity from all angles. I was
then made to reinsert Australia where it originally had
been. I still believed my thoughts were being monitored
by the nurses. This little demon with me was painting
me as some kind of genocidal maniac.

Rescued by Neptune

My most pressing concern was now the tidal waves. This
was damage control. Countless people had already been
killed by the lifting and the dropping of Australia. Now,
there were massive waves headed toward New Zealand

and Japan. Then, it dawned on me to ask Neptune, God of the Seas, for help (on hearing this, the little demon was laughing at me even more, loving just watching me squirm. Initially, I was overjoyed that I'd found a friend. I was also relieved that he could see I wasn't to blame. I told him I was worried about the tidal waves that were fanning out from Australia, repercussions of my previous actions. He said he'd been watching, but had been powerless to help – I had to ask for him. Straight away, he set about cloning himself. Before long, there was a huge circle of Neptunes standing around the upturned Australia, each at the centre of a different tidal wave. Then, they all stomped down their sceptre into the seabed (as gods, they were able to do this). As soon as this happened, the waves all immediately became calm. I was so glad none of Australia's neighbours ended up affected -it was bad enough all the Australians dead. The demon with me now grew furious. He didn't like me thinking for myself and, in the process, becoming exonerated.

I head for Africa

When I thought the worst had passed, the demon by my shoulder made me fly towards Africa. When this happened, my blood ran cold. It seemed that one land mass wasn't enough. Not only would there be some twisted people jealous of my superhuman strength, now they'd think I was a racist as well! Sure enough, I found myself on the east coast of Africa, lifting the country by its beaches like I had before. I felt like scum – but I was again powerless to stop it. Annoyingly, there was no actual way I'd know if anything had happened. I wasn't listening to the news. Would there be a knock at the door and then I'd be arrested? No-one ever came, of course. I was alone in bed at night – in my mind, I would be thinking: how d'you know that the rest of the world hasn't just all died?

Paranoias coming thick and fast

After I told one of my trusted hospital nurses about this, all they had to say was something like:

"It's all in your mind, mate. Don't worry."

Maybe they'd make a joke about it - but never a cruel one. Those one-to-ones always made me feel better. Once I'd vocalised one nightmare, I found that a brand new one would come along, usually the same night. Before long, I was bringing up a different nightmare every one-to-one I had. Part of me felt a little bit proud because I'd created the nightmares myself – but I couldn't really enjoy it. I wasn't controlling my mental experiences – like a kite in a tornado. These days, I don't have these nightmares. At the time, it helped enormously to discuss them with someone with experience of counselling.

Rock bottom

One night, I found an escape. I flew down to the Mariana Trench, over ten kilometres below sea level - the lowest point in the known world. My plan was to fly right down there and hold on to a steel pipe (of my own creation) that stuck out from the floor. When the demon tried to get me to circle the planet and destroy millions more people, I held on to that pipe with all my might. As he focussed on trying to get me to kill, I'd focus on remaining down there.

Mingling with sharks

My mind strayed onto the subject of sharks. The sharks I
was thinking of have a dorsal fin that warns prey of their
presence. I spoke with the sharks' representative about
the fin being a warning. I told him they should swim a
foot or two lower in the water so the fin wouldn't warn of
their presence. My connection was over the moon that I'd
shed light on the problem. A few hours later, he told me
that hundreds of shark attacks right across the world
had resulted in successful kills. In return for the advice I
gave him, my shark contact told me I had a free pass to
swim anywhere I wanted. All the sharks in the world
had orders to leave me alone.

Floating on a polluted lake

At around this time, someone suggested I try creative
visualisation (improving your mood by thinking and
focussing on good thoughts) for the times I felt anxious
or depressed. I should "see myself floating in a rowing
boat on a calm lake". So, I tried. I imagined a beautiful
lake I'd seen photos of in Canada. I saw myself on a boat,
letting the oars rest in their holders. I'd slowly lay back,
trying to enjoy the peace and quiet. That was the idea, at
least. What always happened soon after that was that
the paranoia would take over and engulf me. Every time,
it was the same. I was trying to be calm on my boat, then
long, dark green tentacles started reaching up from the
water around me on my boat. They'd throw the boat from
side-to-side with me fighting to stay on board. Next, I
saw a huge, black storm cloud approaching, with fierce,
noisy lightning flashing underneath it. The final nail in
my coffin was the oil. Thick, black crude appeared from
all the surrounding mountains. The sticky black liquid

would tumble down into the lake from all angles. Each time I experienced the "boat in the lake" I went through the same set of events. That crude oil would eventually kill all the life it flowed over as it headed for me in the middle.

Wrestling with evil

However, many times I tried it, I couldn't get creative visualisation to work. The paranoia would completely take over. Whilst in the grip of it, as well as the terror, it can be very tiring. I started to wonder: what was wrong with me, deep down? Why was I always met with all this evil? I'm just not meant to get stoned. I read somewhere that about one in seven young people who smoke weed will go on to be schizophrenic or be psychotic or suicidal in later life. I know now that I'm the one of those seven who should leave weed well alone – all recreational drugs, frankly. If there had been some kind of clinical test I could have taken before I even tried cannabis, it could have saved a lot of misery and pain.

Try using a crucifix

Another idea I should try when I've got demons in my head was to yell at them (with my thinking voice). This didn't work, either. Yelling at them just made them laugh, and it got even worse. I should picture Jesus Christ on a crucifix, and show him on the cross to the demons. At first, this was working and I felt a bit better. They backed off for a while and I grew hopeful. The next time I tried this (five minutes later) they came back stronger. When they came back, they tore the crucifix from my hands and I saw it burst into flames. I couldn't understand the ferocity with which they treated me. I never thought that deeply inhaling some illegal smoke would lead to such ongoing mental unrest.

Smoke, panic, smoke, repeat

All the torment was plainly bad news, but more so if you knew how often I was daydreaming like this and expanding on those worries. After every smoke break, I returned to my room to daydream. I revelled in having a lockable bedroom door. I sometimes listened to mp3s of (my own) poetry on my phone. I sometimes listened to music. I'd listen to whole albums from start to finish. I did this partly out of respect for the singer or band and partly because an hour was a good length of time between cigarettes.

Police alphabet

Another time, I phoned up the local police station. I asked the police officer who answered about the names of the letters in the police alphabet. I told her I was doing a pub quiz, and that she could help me win. After a bit of pleading, she gave me the whole list. These days you can look things up on the internet, but this was before that was around. At the time, people had to phone people up to find things out. Below is what she told me:

A - ALPHA	N - NOVEMBER
B - BRAVO	O - OSCAR
C - CHARLIE	P - PAPA
D - DELTA	Q - QUEBEC
E - ECHO	R - ROME0
F - FOXTROT	S - SIERRA
G - GOLF	T - TANGO
H - HOTEL	U - UNIFORM
I - INDIA	V - VICTOR
J - JULIET	W - WHISKEY
K - KILO	X - X-RAY
L - LIMA	Y - YANKEE
M - MIKE	Z - ZULU

I memorised the whole list and even used to time myself saying the whole list. I used to be able to recite all the words in mere seconds. And I'd teach anyone willing to listen which word represented which letter.

Career criminal

I met some real fearsome types in hospital. One man told me he was a career criminal. Everyone who met him feared him. If they weren't initially scared, it wouldn't take much for him to change their minds. He said that if he wanted to talk to his crime boss, he'd commit a crime and it'd be arranged that the two of them would share a cell. This way, they could talk about bank jobs or beatings without the authorities getting wind of it. He didn't have a girlfriend. He'd tried having girlfriends in the past, but they were a weakness to him if they were kidnapped. For his sexual needs he always used prostitutes.

Gluttons

This man was very generous with his tobacco. He always called it "burn". He always helped patients who'd just arrived in the hospital; people he'd never met before. At dinner time, though, he'd change completely. He'd sit alone in a corner of the dining area and yell at everyone:

"Gluttons! You're all gluttons! Stuffing your faces. You just want something for free! You lot make me sick. Look at you! Gluttons!"

I'm not sure when he himself ate, but he didn't like us eating much. I've met a lot of the other patients off and on through the years, but I only saw this man once.

So, why are you shaking?

During mealtimes my hands would shake – I was on lithium to keep my mood stable and tremors were a side effect. It was most embarrassing when I tried to eat soup at lunch. I was worried the other patients would think I was shaking with fear and exploit me. In my head, I'd be eagerly transmitting to everyone (I thought was watching) that it was because of the lithium.

If I repeated it enough, hopefully the other people would hear me. Maybe they'd think I was an alcoholic and not just scared? The doctors finally prescribed me some meds to counter the tremors, but this time I'd just dunk the sandwich right in the soup and forget about the spoon. However my performance at lunch went, I'd then return to my room where I could relax a bit and lick my wounds. There, I'd listen to music again and pick up my own private horror show from where it left off.

Winning the argument - at any cost

Sometimes, people would do bizarre things to win fights with nurses, even if they actually came off worse. Some of those things were plain ugly. I walked into the dining area one day and, as usual, there was a patient shouting the odds at staff. An elderly, belligerent patient had been cornered and was screaming threats: "My lawyers..." this, "My lawyers..." that. When the threats no longer registered, she resorted to desperate measures. Right where she was standing, she just pissed on the floor. We all watched agog as a puddle appeared on the floor between her feet. I couldn't believe my eyes and returned to my room to try and block out the image. She really thought she'd taught them a lesson. I think she blamed the staff for her lack of bladder control and played the victim card even more after that.

Outpatients' appointments

Once, in outpatients, I showed up to the meeting with a Diet Coke in my hand (it was a hot day, so I'd bought a cold drink). When I got in the room, the first question they asked was:

"D'you know you're drinking too much caffeine?"

I was flabbergasted. That was the first drink I'd bought all day. And I'd bought it from a vending machine in their own lobby! Another time, as I sat down in the outpatient's meeting, I was asked the weirdest question ever, no sugar-coating.

"How d'you feel about Jews?"

I was shocked. Did I look like I hated Jews? Was there something in my file about me hating Jews? Had I said I hated Jews ages ago while I was ill? Did I look like a Nazi? What was he implying? I took an internal deep breath, quickly composed myself and reassured my CPN that I felt great about Jews, even adding that I had some Jewish friends - which was the truth.

Come across calm

Another time, I'd come straight from the swimming pool. I love the endorphins high you get after you've finished. I even told my CPN (Community Psychiatric Nurse) about it at the time. Then, he asked me:

"You seem quite high today. Could you hazard a guess as to why this is?"

Before the chat I was feeling OK, but that question blind-sided me. While I was still reeling inside, though, I answered another one of his questions. Then, I thought perhaps I should display myself as slightly calmer. So, I tried. Immediately, he registered this change in me and he said:

"You seem a bit flat. I'm concerned. Is something the matter?"

I was furious inside.

Deliberately intrusive questions

During most outpatients' interviews, they'd seize upon the tiniest detail and blow it up into the biggest thing. They only have half an hour to evaluate you, so they might ask deliberately provocative questions. In the early days of my illness, I must've raised some red flags with my answers. I can't remember exactly what my responses were, but they certainly weren't letting me go home. You know you're in trouble when your CPN suddenly excuses himself and leaves the room. He'd stay gone for ages and ages, then he'd reappear with someone else. They'd both walk in with a slight swagger in case things got physical. And, of course, they'd remind you to stay calm:

"You've been formally admitted to such-and-such a hospital, where you'll soon be taken by cab. Your mother has been contacted so she can bring you some clothes and overnight things – she'll meet us there. If you'd like to come with us?" Like I had a choice.

I've never thought of myself as dangerous, but it seemed like they thought I was. It was like I'd been arrested. Usually, I never said a word after hearing their initial declaration of intent.

The belligerent racist

One woman in the hospital was always yelling and swearing at nurses. She was unusually tall, with a stoop and a pot belly of which she was proud. She always smoked Pall Mall cigarettes. The brand always struck me as being poisonously evil somehow, probably because they were this lady's favourite. I used to think I could smell something odd if a Pall Mall cigarette was being smoked nearby. To hear her speak, it was effing black this, effing black that. She seemed to almost relish using the n- word and the c- word, and these words were always louder than the others. She only spoke quietly when it was about money. She'd often be ranting for so long that her cigarette would turn to ash. This ash would always somehow remain attached to her cigarette, albeit in a slightly drooping shape. She was married to the man who'd scrounge and scavenge for dog-ends and yell between wards to this woman. Because I'd heard there were torture tunnels under the old hospital, maybe there were tunnels under the new one, too?

Old woman gone

Then one day, this disruptive old woman vanished. Of course, I thought she'd finally been taken down to the tunnels. I was in my bed with my music being bombarded with images of her in the sinister dark and wet down there. I could see all the nurses exacting their revenge on this woman. She was getting hurt for every time she'd been racist, every patient she'd betrayed, every man she'd tried to ply with tobacco - all her cruelties. I pictured her on a chair alone down there, where a nurse had stuffed a gag into her mouth.

Fountains of blood

Now the nurses were betting amongst themselves. How high would her blood squirt when they got around to slitting her jugular artery? Some estimated as much as ten feet, but in the end, the blood squirted only about six. After the body had been disposed of (easy when you're in a hospital) the nurses who'd tortured and killed her took a couple of weeks off for a relaxing holiday. The directors of the hospital trust themselves had sanctioned these actions, including the torture. The racist woman had been a pest every time she'd been in the hospital (which was once every eighteen months or so). Her admissions had started thirty or forty years ago. All this time, she'd been feigning illness and claiming thousands and thousands of pounds worth of bogus benefits. Every patient I knew secretly wanted her dead. Every nurse wanted her dead. I never spoke to anyone about any of this, of course. I thought if I said something, I'd be dragged down to the tunnels and slaughtered next.

Mealtime superstitions

Whenever I eat a meal and there's meat on the plate, I always feel I should try a bit of the meat first. If I don't, it's like I've broken some kind of rule. Sometimes, I eat the sprouts first, then the egg, then the pork, or the bubble and squeak, then the lamb (although not in the same meal). It doesn't apply to seafood. When I'm eating surrounded by other people, I used to really worry. If someone was sitting over to the right, and I ate something on the right of the plate – facing their way - that person might get upset. Likewise, if I ate some beans, or whatever, from the left side of the plate, someone over in that direction could get upset. I know this is just overthinking, but sometimes I'd create these worries for myself and still be tangled up in them for a long time afterwards.

The cut on my wrist

One morning, in the hospital, I woke up with a small, unexplained cut across my left wrist. You could barely see it. I couldn't understand how it had gotten there. Then, it hit me - one of the girls had tried to kill me in my sleep. Her plan was to seduce me, then stab me to death, but I was too strong. We'd both fought, then I'd disarmed her and took the knife. Then, because I wanted to show her that I was impervious to pain, I made a mark on my wrist while she watched. After that, she ran off and I fell back asleep.

Why's she drinking Coke?

The next day, I tried to act natural when I saw her. Deep down, I still thought she feared me. I even felt sympathy. She'd failed her Mafia bosses and now they'd punish her. That following day, this girl was drinking Coca-Cola. In the three weeks I'd known her, I'd never seen her drink Coca-Cola. To my mind, the bottle was red like the Devil. It was the drink of a killer and all my theories were true!

Another cut on my wrist

The next morning, I saw another scratch on my arm next to the first. I knew I'd been attacked, by a different girl. It had been an exact repeat of the night before. I now started thinking the nurses had been giving me extra-strong meds. They wanted me to be asleep while I'm stabbed to death. The way I saw it, very powerful people wanted me dead. The nurses had given both the girls sharp knives (scalpels even?), then told them to go and get me. It hadn't occurred to me that the nurses could easily just overmedicate me and throw me into the tunnels. I thought about those murder attempts for months afterwards. After my few days of sheer terror (ironically in the observation room right next to the nurses' control room for extra safety), I was put in a regular room with a lock and the scars soon went.

The Geographer wants me dead

As far as I could make out, there was a huge price on my head. It had been put there by that darkest, most evil of figureheads: The Geographer. His name came from the fact that all of his followers, right across the world and in real time could feel the aftershocks of his orgasms, and often acknowledged them with a sip of some liquid or other. He was the known God of Sounds. He supplied arms, equipment and fuel to all sides of any conflict or unrest – local or global. He's the ultimate spiritual king of criminals – almost worse than the king of manipulation through fear: Satan. The Geographer is controlling all the ultimate bad guys you've ever seen in films, read about in books or heard of in news stories. Rumour had it he snorted super pure cocaine mixed with freeze-dried baby's blood when he wanted a thrill. The Geographer was so powerful, he controlled even luck itself.

£400 for a room key

Towards the end of that month after I saw the little scars on my arm, I asked for a one-to-one with a nurse so I could get my worries off my chest. I told the nurse I thought such-and-such a patient was paying £400 to such-and-such a nurse for a door key to my room. After I told that nurse, she just laughed – I'd chosen the wrong nurse in this case. She told me there's no way the patient I was worried about could afford £400 for a key. At the time, I remember thinking she'd totally missed the point, but I had to make sense of her humour. And after a tortured and fraught struggle trying not to believe it, I forgot all about it.

And the penny drops

One of the other patients (Jim) in the hospital used to really bother me. But, I felt so wretched at the time that I thought I deserved the torment. He'd walk about wearing the same round sunglasses that John Lennon used to wear. He'd usually be droning on about some global conspiracy theory. Then, when he'd narrowed it down to only one possible culprit for the latest terrorist attack, wanting you to vocalise the obvious, he'd deliver his catchphrase "…And the penny drops." On that rather patronising bombshell, he'd sweep grandly off to his room for a while, or make himself some coffee. If everyone else called you Matt, he'd call you Matthew. If everyone else called you Katie, he'd call you Katherine. He was the kind of man you wanted to keep onside whilst in hospital, but outside, not so much.

Evading Jim

The last time I saw this man, it was in a convenience store. He came in and I darted off and hid down an aisle. I think he terrorised this shopkeeper quite frequently 'cos this is what he said:

"…Take, for example, the T1000 from Terminator 2. It's a killer robot. Totally immune to bullets. Its whole *raison d'être*, if you will, is to follow orders and kill people. Now, those high-up in the western military-industrial complex have known about this technology for years. Who d'you think's out there in Kosovo/ Iraq/ Syria fighting America's wars with no American casualties? Killer robots, that's who."

Shopkeeper – playing along: "I see."

Jim: "…And the penny drops." With that, of course, he sweeps grandly out of the shop to pester someone else who's also not able to leave first.

Are you in or out?

It was often strange, returning to the hospital as an

outpatient. All the other patients would want to hear
tales of how you were getting stoned or drunk every
night, having sex or doing crimes. This was mainly
because they were things they'd like to be doing. If I had
to go back to the hospital to visit friends, I'd hate it.
Once, a nurse even said this to me:

"Hey! How are you doing? Are you in, or out?"

He was, of course, claiming not to know if I was resident
there or just visiting. That scared me. I always used to
ask that nurse to brush my teeth for me while I was
there, so he was still sore from that. Still, it chilled me to
the bone when he asked. These days, if I have to see a
friend who's an inpatient, I'll plan a meeting far from the
hospital, if possible. That nurse had flippantly asked me
a question, feigning concern. And, of course, it was quite
condescending.

System healthy

When the alarm went off for a patient emergency in the
hospital, all the nurses leapt into action. They'd hear the
alarm, and one of them would check the little, blue
screen which was in the main hallway which told them
where the trouble was. They'd then tell the other nurses
and they'd all head off in that direction. You could hear
their keys all jangling about as even the slower nurses
ran about. You could sometimes see them quickly trying
to unlock the doors between them and the trouble spot.
Often, it had sounded because a patient had fallen over
on the elderly ward. Outside of these brief, panicky
times, that blue screen just read "system healthy". I
loved reading that phrase as I'd walk past quietly. I felt
as if my system was healthy, as well.

Tasting blood

I've never really tried self-harm myself, except for a couple of times. The first time, I was in hospital, thinking about my Dad. He'd just moved to another country and I wanted to reach out to him somehow. I thought that I could do this through feeling physical pain. I wanted him to feel it, but at the same time I didn't want to hurt him. Maybe I thought he'd feel a light tingle on his body where I'd felt the real pain? So, I opened a tin of beans I'd smuggled in and got hold of the very sharp, curled-up, detached metal lid. With the lid, I hacked into my arm, hard and fast. I did this for another reason, as well, which was just beyond stupid: I wanted to taste my own blood.

Bruce Lee

I'd grown up on Bruce Lee films, and was a big fan. In one of his films, at the end, he's in a fight with the boss. At one point, this Boss cuts Bruce Lee's chest with his sharpened claws. Bruce Lee takes a moment and dabs at the cut with his fingers. He tastes the blood and this makes him angrier/ fight better. I'd wondered ever since then if tasting my own blood would make me angry, as well. So, I slashed into my arm with the sharp piece of metal. I tasted the blood and remember thinking it tasted metallic. It hadn't made me angry, though, like it had with Bruce Lee. It had probably made him angry in the film because his opponent had caused the bleeding. That hadn't even crossed my mind at the time. I still have a small scar from that.

Clipper smiley scar

Another scar that remains from the same time is when I burned myself. If you spark a Clipper lighter and leave it burning for a while, the metal around the top becomes hot. Once it's almost red hot, you press it onto your, or your friend's, hand. The usual place for this is on the hand between your first finger and the base of the thumb, in the crook of the L-shape. This was supposed to be an initiation ritual. In the hospital, though, there was only me, but I still went ahead with it. The resulting scar is supposed to look like a little smiley face – while burning hot, the two sides of the metal wheel formed the eyes and the U-shaped flame guard left the smile. Of course, I made a mess of it, and now I've got a small, blob-shaped scar on my hand instead.

I burn myself with a cigarette

Not five minutes later, I started at my other hand. I'd read that some gangs in America use this as an initiation ritual. You had to hold a lit cigarette onto your arm until it burned down all the way to the filter. At the time, of course, I was alone and no-one had made me do it. I'd seen other patients in the hospital run a lighter flame across their forearm so you could smell the burning hairs, but never holding a lit cigarette like that. When I tried this on myself, it hurt like hell. The cigarette on my arm didn't leave a scar, I removed it before I did any real damage. It seemed a perfectly normal thing to do at the time.

Four poems

I was given two whole hours leave from the hospital. I

was excited as I jumped down the stairs four at a time. My mind was full of all the great things I was going to do. I was going to go to my flat and type up two of my more recent poems and smoke cigarettes - in complete peace and quiet. Then a psychiatrist walked by up ahead of me, and through a door to another ward. I heard one of his shoes brushing against the floor as he walked. He didn't know I was there, but the message to me was crystal clear. I interpreted the brushing sound to be:

"If you don't type up *four* poems today when you go back to your flat, you will be ended."

I fail the test

I tried to stay calm after I heard this fearsome message but it had shaken me to the core. I wanted to type up some poems anyway, but four would be really pushing it. Each was a hand-written side of A4, so they weren't what you'd call short poems. It was going to be difficult to do four. So now I had a fire under me, instead of waiting for the bus, I ran to my flat. I ran for what would have been seven or eight bus-stops, in the rain. In the end, when I reached my flat, I only managed to type up three poems. Given that this was now life or death, I was willing to try to stretch my time off the ward. I had to finish all four. Then, I got a phone call from a ward nurse. He said I had to come back to the hospital immediately. I really felt all these things were linked. I was only about five minutes over my time at that point. Usually, they give you about an hour before they chase you up. Since the threat had been communicated to me from the sound of a *doctor*'s shoe dragging, it was extra official and sanctioned from on high. I thought it only natural that a nurse (in collusion with the foot scuffing doctor) would want to rush me and treat me so unfairly. Put simply, they all wanted me to fail.

Rubble through the window

I think I should tell you about my flat. While I wasn't there, I'd dream up some outlandish situations. Further examples of the intrusive thoughts common to the mentally ill – although where exactly they intrude from is still officially unknown. One of these was that there were dozens of rioters with burning torches congregating and smashing down my door. I could clearly see them all running up my stairs and taking my stuff. Then, they'd burn the flat to the ground. I was always surprised that when I went back there, on leave, no rioters had broken in and things were just how I'd left them. Sometimes, I'd think that one of my own family had let the burglars in, which would void any claims I might make on my insurance since there was no forced entry. One time, I saw a dump truck filled with builder's rubble floating just outside my flat. I could see it hovering outside the window. Then, the whole rear part of it raised up and all the rubble came crashing through the windows and into my lounge and bedroom, wrecking everything. My flat is two floors up from street-level, so this could never actually happen. But if you believed in magic like I used to, life could get quite peculiar. If you're not present watching something magical happen, how do you know it didn't happen? I was accidentally angering all sorts of supremely powerful gods and devils at the time and magic was a normal thing.

My family are my worst enemy

I didn't trust my family. This was probably because they were the only ones left not to trust. When I was ill, I'd been insulting other people for ages. I didn't even trust my own Mum. It must've been soul-destroying for her at the time - I was very ill. I then asked her to give me her copies of my flat keys. I wanted to make sure I had both copies with me. There weren't any other copies anywhere else in the world, as far as I knew. For a short time, I considered my family my worst enemies. They'd done nothing to deserve this. The mistrust was a manifestation of my paranoia and I considered them all monsters.

Coughs of urgency

One day, I overheard somebody speaking on the phone. He was talking to his friend, but something hit me (I'd already decided that this man was in the Mafia and now, I was certain). He said:

"I'll see you in two months."

This sounds regular, but that wasn't the whole story. He'd cleared his throat just before he said, "two months." I was certain it was Mafia code. Another time, I'd heard someone else (another Mafioso) on the phone. He had also coughed before saying a period of time. The way I saw it, if you cough, it brings the time forward by an increment. So, "two months" comes to mean "two weeks". This code only worked over the phone, though. It was a way to confuse the authorities, if they were bugging the call. As another example, if I said:

"I'll meet you in two days." That's just what I meant. But if I said:

"I'll meet you in *coughs* two days." This means that I'll meet you in two hours. You had to cough just before saying the time increment. So:

Years *coughs* becomes *months*;

Months *coughs* becomes *weeks;*

Weeks *coughs* becomes *days*;

Days *coughs* becomes *hours*, and so on.

I'm not sure if minutes became seconds, but if they did, that'd be a very urgent phone conversation to hear.

Mafia phone calls

I always thought those conversations were always about criminal or violent things. After I'd heard who I thought was a Mafioso on the phone, I'd be worried for hours after that. Of course, I wouldn't trust the person who'd been talking, and (if I was paying attention) the same went for their visitors. It got much worse when I was given one of the double rooms. While I wasn't sharing with a Mafioso, the patients' phone was right outside the door. From my bed, I could hear most people talking on the phone (and tactically coughing) loud and clear.

Olive technique

I thought that when Mafiosi talked while eating olives, a great deal depended on how the olives were eaten. If you appreciated the gravity of the other person's statement, it was customary to eat two or more olives at once. If the Mafioso you're talking to says:

"It's a beautiful day" and you responded by eating a single olive: you showed yourself to be quite naïve.

If the Mafioso says:

"It's a beautiful day today," (but you knew that he meant "…a beautiful day to get away with murder") and you put two or more olives in your mouth, then it was understood that a murder was intended. Of course, a true olive lover would always eat the olive, swallow the flesh of it, then swallow the pits, but that was a given. Of course, if the person across from you ate their olives, then spat out the pits? You were being insulted - or the eater was just naïve. Based on my theory of olive consumption by organised criminals, I always carefully observed the other people when I shared out my olives. Anybody who ate two or more at the same time immediately went on my Mafia watch list.

Official crying

I thought that Italians would cry unreservedly when something was emotional. Further to this, the unwritten rule was that "at least one tear" would have to roll down the person's cheek for it to be a proper emotional moment. This was especially important if the killer of a man was present at that man's funeral and he wanted to convince everyone of his innocence. If the tears welled up in his eye and no tear went down the cheek, it didn't count and he'd be conspicuously unmoved. If at least one tear flowed down his face, though, he'd be off the hook and he'd passed the crucial test. Around Italian people (or those I even suspected of being Italian or even of knowing how to speak some Italian in some cases) I was conscious of these factors. It was never an exact science, but I know I didn't like it. Sometimes, I'd eat as many as six or more olives at one time and then swallow all the pits, but I was only pretending to be dangerous.

Almost poisoned by burglars

On leave once to my flat, I saw my kitchen shelf had
collapsed. It was a burglar! That burglar had also
poisoned my crumpled Coke bottle. For some reason, I
tasted the liquid inside and it tasted putrid. I was so
convinced it contained a poison that I ran straight to the
toilet and threw up. I was fighting for my life. I really
don't know much about poisons, but I thought I was
dealing here with arsenic. I thought that if arsenic was
bad, strychnine was far worse. I thought that arsenic
had to be ingested to kill you, but strychnine could be
fatal just by touching your skin.

Rational explanations

Some while afterwards, I realised I'd crumpled the Coke
bottle myself. Although it looks like you've messed with
the bottle for no reason, it was something some
bartenders do. The less space there is above the liquid
sealed in the bottle, the better. Less space means the
carbon dioxide is forced to remain as bubbles in the
liquid for longer. I also concluded that the shelf collapsed
because I'd put too many heavy things on it. The nasty
taste in my mouth from drinking from the bottle must've
just been old, out-of-date Coke or my mind playing
tricks.

X-ray vision for poisons

Still thinking a burglar was trying to poison me, I
returned cautiously to the hospital. Now, though, I had
developed a new superpower. I had X-ray vision which
showed me poisons. More specifically, I could see food
that'd been laced with poison. If I was looking at a beef

burger, and there was a yellow glow around it, it had arsenic in it. If a sausage roll or sandwich had a purple glow around it, it had strychnine in it. Back in the hospital, I saw a yellow glow around all the food the nurses were serving everyone from the hatch. I was forced to stop eating with the other patients completely. None of the other patients eating the food were collapsing and dying because they'd all been given the antidote while I was away briefly on leave. This was why the poison wasn't killing them and they could eat the poisoned food safely. I, on the other hand, had to live on crisps from the vending machine for a while – for safety's sake.

Poisoned cigarettes

Soon, I started thinking that my brand of cigarettes had also been laced with arsenic. I still believed that people right across the world absolutely hated me. Rich people, poor people, black, white, men, women, *everyone* wanted me dead. I'd just been formally excommunicated by God and the Devil to suffer eternally and now I felt persecuted, claustrophobic and alone. They'd poisoned the cigarettes I bought, so smoking would kill me, too. Of course, all the people smoking my brand had been given the antidote earlier. Since only one arsenic cigarette wouldn't kill me, I thought maybe it was a cumulative thing. Strangely, even considering the Geographer's vast resources, strychnine wasn't used on the smokes I bought. I was told that it cost too much.

The table tennis nurse

Playing ping pong or table tennis in the hospital could be good fun – unless you kept getting beaten. One of the

nurses was amazing. Just the way he gripped the bat in
his hand told you he meant business. Everything, right
down to his serve, was awe-inspiring to watch. Whenever
he served, he'd throw the ball high up into the air. When
it came down, he'd hit the ball and stamp his foot at the
same time. The ball (often with excessive topspin) would
then curve tightly through the air, clearing the net by
mere inches. His shots would always be just about
clipping the back and side edges of the table the other
side – almost consistently unreachable for the poor
person playing him. If you were up against him, you had
to stand quite a way back from the table if you wanted a
chance of hitting the ball back. His returns and smashes
could be so violent that he'd frequently demolish his
opponent. There were two big, psychological hits that
you took when you played this man. Firstly: when you're
left standing with your mouth open after one of his
breath-taking winners you doubt your own skill - not as
fast, not as accurate. And secondly, there's the
humiliation of having to go and seek out the ball.

Second-hand medication

One time, I was alone in one of the hospital lounges. I
was watching something on TV in between cigarettes.
Then two patients walked in and started whispering. It
turned out that the doctors had put the first one on some
meds and the second one wanted to buy them from him.
After a little while, they shook on their deal and left. At
evening meds later, I carried out an experiment. I held
some blue lorazepam in my mouth at the meds hatch,
walked quickly away and spat it out in my room. All that
remained on my windowsill was blue mush. The
company that made lorazepam must have allowed for

this. It was quite a powerful drug, so they'd made it powdery so it was hard to smuggle in the moisture of your mouth. I'd never be able to sell what I'd smuggled. I concluded that the two patients I'd seen dealing weren't trading lorazepam tablets.

Smarties

James, in the hospital, was always trying to smuggle his meds (he'd also tried lifting me into a bin earlier, we weren't friends). After the nurse had given him his meds, he always tried to scurry off and get rid of the pills somehow. He'd always be moaning that the nurses didn't have the right to make him take the meds (although I think they did). Whenever meds time came around, he was always first in line. He usually wanted to show the nurses how willing and compliant he was. After they'd been dispensed to him, he'd pause with his mouth open - demonstrating that he'd swallowed everything. Then, he'd swiftly walk off. After a little while, the nurses cottoned on. Straight after he'd put the pills in his mouth, they'd ask him a simple question. Of course, he couldn't talk and hide his meds at the same time. I was glad they caught him, he wasn't well-liked. He always referred to meds as "Smarties". He was one of the few people I met in the mental health system that I'd say was institutionalised. It didn't seem to matter to him how long he was locked away. He'd attack a nurse/ patient/ visitor just to extend his stay on the ward.

Diamond Eyes

I was in my flat and I made a new friend. There was a housefly in the flat with me. I closed all the windows so he couldn't fly off. Whenever I thought the insect was angry, I'd consider him Baron Greenback – the baddie from Danger Mouse. I'd call to him telepathically like he was a dog or cat as he buzzed past me now and then. Mine was a one bedroom flat, so he flew past me quite often. Whenever I thought the fly was being friendly towards me, I called him Diamond Eyes – because they have hundreds of eyes. That fly's mood swings between the two extremes came thick and fast, as you may expect. I had some breath mints. I took one out, and licked the sugary food so Baron Greenback would smell it, land on it and start eating it. Almost immediately, he found it and started sucking away at it with his mouthparts.

Baron Greenback

This was the only time I kept a fly as a pet. They tend to just buzz around and not really say much, except for the buzzing sound, and then the lack of sound when they've stopped buzzing. The mood swings were also a big, off-putting factor. I knew that my fly had started life as a maggot. So, then I started thinking that if I'd known Diamond Eyes as a maggot, would he have been easier to train? I'm only joking. Someone else can do that research. After half an hour trying to get some sense out of Diamond Eyes/ Baron Greenback, I opened a window and he disappeared.

Ward-based suicide attempt

I've met a few people who've tried suicide by hanging. Quite often, they were even willing to prove it by showing you the scars on their neck. One person had tried to get run over by a bus, but they spotted him with his head by the tyre in the nick of time. I've tried suicide a few times, and once when I was still in the hospital – by cutting. I'd borrowed a razor to shave during a bath. Once I was in the hot water, I tried slashing at my neck, and wrists until the water turned orange. I thought I was doing the right thing and that suicide was the only way of sparing my family. I was in a right state, as you can imagine.

I melt my belt

Another time, I'd just arrived at the hospital and I was wearing a long, black, plastic belt. I wanted it shorter, but had nothing with which to cut it. Then I decided to melt off part of it. I got my lighter and started burning. The plastic quickly became molten and this dripped onto the floor. I also sprayed deodorant all over the window. Later, I felt guilty about the black plastic puddle on the floor. Once it had cooled down, the cleaners really couldn't remove that stain.

Working for the Pope

So, I was daydreaming in the hospital and I had a direct connection with The Vatican in Rome. I was talking to the Bishop who oversaw clandestine spells. These were some ancient, horrifyingly powerful spells. This man worked for the Pope in a secret library deep beneath the Vatican – and it was full of hundreds of massive, dusty spell books. No-one officially even knew he was there. The scenario was this: the Italian Bishop would find an old spell book and read that Latin spell out loud. This would summon up a demon from far below the earth in hell. It would then surface somewhere in the world. It was my job to then do two things. First, I had to locate the demon; and, second, I had to create a cage in which it could be contained forever.

I find and restrain the demon

So, I'd hear the Bishop read out the spell and quickly assume my position. I'd start orbiting the earth in readiness, I had to be observing the entire earth. Then, I'd find the demon that'd just been released - it'd be obvious to me, somehow - and I'd return to earth to restrain it. Once I'd cajoled it into a temporary cage, I knew I had about twenty minutes and then the real work began. It's worth noting that this incarceration always infuriated the creatures as I dealt with them. They'd be spouting vitriol and curses at me and rattling the cage, while I'm considering the elements required for a more permanent cage. Each demon's cage required a specific blend of different elements.

Bespoke cages

So, I'd make manifest a smaller cage within the original cage. I started with adamantium - the bars, floor and ceiling all made of that material. If he breaks out, I'd try an alloy of iron and adamantium, put that around the demon and see if he could break out. If that failed, gold and adamantium, silver and adamantium, and so on. I had the entire periodic table at my disposal – which was a blessing and a curse. All the while, I was pressed for time. I had to devise a sturdy, bespoke cage for whichever demon it was in the twenty minutes from when it'd first surfaced. If I failed in my task, whichever demon it was would be unleashed upon an unsuspecting world and it'd be my fault. The Bishop understood that I could only process one demon at a time, and so he timed the next spell-reading accordingly. It was tiring work because it required such intense concentration.

God's blessing

The work could also get quite scary, what with the demon screaming and cursing me and bursting into flames. A bit like the twisting I mentioned earlier, it was very reassuring to have God's blessing behind everything you were doing. At the time, I was hearing lots of Latin words coming from the Bishop (and some from the trapped demons). I wish I'd written down some of those words at the time, to check if they were real Latin. Even if the Latin used in the spells *was* real, I wouldn't suggest any of this as a pastime for anyone. It was tiring and risky. If the deadline for a permanent cage went by and the demon was still free, the fate of the good people of the world was on the line. The demons I was dealing with were fierce and fearless. If one of them went on a killing spree and went after my family, the church was safe. The Vatican would deny everything and say that the entire thing was the fabrication of a mental person.

Floridian weed

So, in the hospital, one of the other patients had got hold of some strong weed. He said it'd come from Florida, on America's east coast. It was by far the strongest stuff I'd ever smoked – and I used to smoke a lot of weed. After he gave me the fat joint he'd already rolled, he warned me not to smoke the whole thing in one go. His words went in one ear and out the other. I didn't think of myself as new to this *although, of course, I did have a recurring habit of being sectioned and trying to kill myself after the first time I got stoned – and after every time I got stoned since then. Tragically for me, I still saw getting high as being cool and popular, and not psychosis-inducing and capable of bringing on such paranoia that I'd want to die there and then,* so I went full steam ahead. It turned out he was right - it was powerful stuff. I was feeling strange after smoking the first half of it, so, strategically, I let the rest of the joint go out. I wanted to have it later. Illogically, I was still treating the destructive substance as a delicacy.

Stoned hitmen

I hid the last half of that powerhouse joint in my glasses case, which ended up making things worse. After I'd put the joint in there, my illness revved up again. Every man in glasses that I saw come into the hospital after that was a hit man working for the Mafia. I thought that because I'd kept my weed in with my glasses, hundreds of killers had done the same. This had led to lots of stoned hit men running about – all over the world. They were all getting stoned before they left, on the way to kill whomever it was. They'd arrive at the location, see the target and start hugging him, running about crazily, getting the munchies and messing everything up. Now, the Mafia and shadow governments had overnight lost millions of pounds. Everyone knew it was my fault and they knew where I was staying. I wanted the earth to open and swallow me before any of them could reach me and do worse.

Chessboard head

Soon enough, like a total twat, I smoked the rest of that joint from my glasses case. It felt like the best thing to do. I waited 'til late in the evening when most people were asleep and sparked it up. I took that smoke down into my lungs, deep as ever – I used to be such a sensible chap! Before long, I was more stoned than I'd ever been. My head turned into a police siren's light, and I thought everyone could see it flashing - even through walls and doors. If I thought about it hard enough, I could change the light into different colours, although that took a lot of concentration. Then, my mind changed into a chess board, complete with the pieces in position in 3D with pieces taking other pieces. I was all fucked up. I was over the moon the next day when my head went back to being just my head again.

My Joe Pesci moment

One time, I was angry with the world. I've been bullied in the past, and I know how bad it feels. Even so, I walked out onto the smoking pod furious. I saw another patient there who'd been a resident a bit longer than I had. I was younger than him, but he was taller. I approached him and stood with my nose barely a foot away from his. I was a problem. I could see his cigarette pack poking out a bit from his shirt pocket and reached up towards it. Still holding his gaze, I got the box and took a cigarette. I told him:

"This is mine".

What about Ron?

To my core I believed that the cigarette belonged to me, he'd just been keeping it for me. He was scared stiff. At the time, I was psychotic. After I'd sparked up the cigarette I took, he went to leave. But I stopped him:

"What about Ron?" I asked.

"Who's Ron?" he said.

"Later on." I said, and calmly took a second cigarette.

"That wasn't so hard now, was it?"

Then I slapped him gently on the face. I was acting like Joe Pesci in Goodfellas! This was all out of character for me. A few weeks later, I regretted my actions toward him back then in the pod. In my defence, I had really no idea what I was doing. It got to the point after that where the poor man would only go out onto the pod to smoke with one cigarette in his box. By doing that, if I wanted to take another one from him, he could say it was his last one. By now, I let these lies slide. I knew he must've had more cigarettes in his room, but I didn't bring it up - even my cruel side had its limits.

The U2 fan

There was a man, in the hospital at the same kind of time, who was a massive fan of the Irish rock group U2. Every day, he'd sit himself down in the non-smoking room on the big sofa facing the TV. He didn't hang out with any of the groups in the hospital as it was, mainly because he didn't smoke. He watched the same U2 DVD over and over. It was about one of the band's tours somewhere. Every day, he watched the same DVD. No-one liked him, but, on balance, he wasn't really annoying anyone.

Scuffle in the lunch queue

In the lunch queue one day, things were more tense than usual on the ward. The U2 fan was queueing right behind me and he must've touched my back or something. Out of the blue, I turned to face him and burst into song. He told me to shut up and pushed me away. I shook it off and pushed him harder. He fell backwards onto the cutlery trolley and then the floor, and couldn't get up. A gang of about four other male patients immediately threw him across the floor and under the lunch counter. While he was still down on the floor, they began kicking and punching him. Then there was a lot of argy-bargy and the main attack alarm went off. After what seemed like ages, the nurses got the U2 fan to safety and talked everyone down. Then, the police arrived. The four attackers were called into the nurses' room individually, so they couldn't confer and agree on a false series of events. Even though I'd officially started the fight, the police didn't want to talk to me. This was probably because I hadn't stomped on the man while he was on the floor.

The bugged pedometer

A day or two later, the man I'd been bullying for smokes had a visit from his parents. His Mum brought him his usual stuff: more cigarettes; get well cards from family friends. Also, she had something for me. I think it was meant as a peace offering. It was a small, red pedometer. If I fixed it to my belt, it would count how many steps I was walking every day. This, in turn, would help me get back into shape. I think she'd got it free with breakfast cereal. I took the gift and thanked her. I wasn't sure why she'd given it to me at first. Some batty, old woman thinking I was too fat, handing me a bit of crummy plastic? She wanted her son to have a smoother ride with me around and thought calling me fat like this would help? Then, I connected the dots. It was a listening device. She and her handlers must think I'm a complete moron! I'd never catch on to what it really was. I'd just attach it to my belt and they'd hear all my secrets and tell-tale noises I made as I lived my life. It was designed so The Geographer's people could keep an eye on me, steal my best ideas and crumple my ambitions.

Suspicious remote

I quickly worked through these thoughts and waited until she left the room. Then, I stamped on this small, red piece of evil. I stomped and stomped until it was in many pieces on the floor. From that point on, I couldn't trust anything electronic or portable. A few seconds later, I found another bug. This time, it was hidden inside the TV remote control. I took that apart as well, stomping on it until it was totally broken. This marked the start of my glitter bugs phase. A few groups of powerful people were trying to hear what I was doing. Not only would they be *hearing* me and the sounds I made, they'd also be *listening to my thoughts*. Soon, I became aware that individual pieces of metallic glitter were listening devices. Each piece of glitter (whichever colour it was) had a small microphone and a small but powerful transmitter inside it. It didn't help that most glitter you can buy is a tiny hexagon shape - a sure fire clue that something involving advance technology is at play. I thought the technology had only just been developed by the very greatest scientists, but it was being kept from the public for a few more years. These were tiny, electronic devices that can record people's thoughts. It was undisputable fact and I knew it to be true.

Glitter bugs

In a glitter-bugged room, I was under heavy surveillance. Someone would be listening to me from a secret control room hidden somewhere miles underground. To add insult to injury, I was then finding them everywhere. Then, I thought I'd seen someone duck quickly out of my bedroom while I was out smoking. I knew he wouldn't have stolen anything – he'd have put a glitter bug in there. What upset me more was that he'd dropped that tiny, intrusive device deliberately down the back of my radiator. He knew full well that I'd never be able to get to it once there. Even so, I quickly forgave him. One of his handlers must've made him do it. All the other public rooms had already been glitter-bugged as far as I was concerned, so mine would have been bugged soon anyway.

Attack by greetings card

Then, one of the older patients made me a greetings card in OT. My room was already dirty, but I knew where the bugs were. Someone then brought me the card the lady had made. Harmless enough, you would have thought. Still, I opened the envelope, found the card inside and nearly choked with horror as I opened it to read it. Hundreds of red and silver glitter bugs, a sea of them, spilled out of the card and all over the floor. The card was coated - inside and out. Even this polite, soft-spoken lady was working for The Geographer. No-one was safe. It would take ages to clear up every individual piece. The instant the glitter came flooding out of the card, I was furious with the old lady – we'd only spoken once, if that. But then I reflected on things and concluded that her handler must've forced her to be that cruel. Someone working for someone working for The Geographer probably had threatened her grandchildren or something to make her attack me like she did.

Glitter bugs in ward round

It took me quite a while to concede that there were too many glitter bugs in my room to tidy up. It was too bad that I had to sleep in there, but I had to roll with the punches. So, being careful not to drop any more of the evidence, I took that card along with me into my next ward round. If the doctor could see for himself the scale of the surveillance I had to deal with every day, he'd understand my problem and want to help. All he had to do was take even just one of the glitter bugs to a lab like I wanted him to. The tests would confirm they were next generation surveillance devices and it'd prove I was right to be fearful. We were talking about hundreds of tiny, state-of-the-art recording devices monitoring an innocent civilian. Something had to be done.

Wearing or eating a glitter bug

Now, I was most worried about having a glitter bug stuck to my clothes somewhere, or even eating one by mistake. If I was carrying a glitter bug around with me, it wouldn't matter if the room was bugged or not; I'd personally be bugged. Soon, I'd filled in the backstory to these glitter bugs. There were five different groups all tuning in to me and they would act quickly if they thought I was becoming any kind of threat to them.

The five groups

While my mind was still reeling, I was moved into

another room. The first thing I did was to sweep the new room for glitter bugs. To do this, I'd take some deep breaths and stay quiet for a little while. If there was a glitter bug in there with me, I could sense it. I, bizarrely, could locate singular glitters at around this time, which only served to feed into my problem. I found five, and I assessed that they were each from different groups. There was one by the curtains, one by the cupboard, one under the bed, one on the table, and one by the mirror. I put them all together on a bar of white soap by the sink so I wouldn't lose any. Those groups, if upset by something I'd said or thought, would then issue the order to attack (which I'd hear about telepathically). Usually, it would be aimed at someone close to me. People like my family and friends were often given as targets. The groups annoying me were a strange but powerful selection. There were:

- the Hell's Angels
- the Knights Templar
- the Metropolitan Police
- the Sicilian Mafia and
- the Illuminati

The groups attack

All it would take was a single, slightly angry thought, and there'd be an attack. How was I to know if something had happened outside the ward? In my head I would hear "move on his brother," "move on his father," or something like that. If I'd thought to myself that there was a better place to grow lemons than Sicily, I'd hear "move on his mother." Obviously, this would've come from the Sicilian group (and I've made up the insult, but you get the idea). The first group to order a "move on [someone]" was the Hell's Angels. After that, all the other groups started using the same phrase. Given the size and the collective power of the groups represented, I found those all-five bugged rooms really frightening. If I walked into a clean room, I loved it. I was relatively happy in rooms like that. I could sense the bugs, strangely. The nurses, doctors, my friends and my family couldn't really understand, but they were patient and tried to help.

No such thing

Life in the hospital meant lots of smoking. There'd be a visit now and then, and then back to the smoking. Sometimes, I thought of smoking as suicidal. Another ongoing worry was that my Mum had been murdered – while off the ward. It was usually carried out by one of the groups having me surveilled. They were so powerful that they were above the law –everyone knew they'd get away with it. I'd be there in the smoking-room smoking, but I'd be thinking about how my Mum had just been murdered. I'd heard that the order in my head had gone out to "move on his Mum" because of something I'd thought in a dirty room. Then, I had to ignore all the voices because I'd see her *walking towards me* through the smoking-room windows – at exactly the time we'd arranged for a visit. She always looked pretty and confident – but, inside, I was always shocked. I'd smile and carefully leave the room. My Mum's meetings were always pleasant – depending on the severity of my illness at the time. Furthermore, each time her visit came around, her being alive and well meant that everything I'd been thinking and worried about(notably her being killed) had been completely unfounded. Again, when she left, my extreme mental agitation would only pick up from where it left off.

Stay of execution

Frankly, I didn't know what to think. I knew I was pleased to see her, but I wasn't sure how she'd managed to stay alive. I then found myself starting to lose faith in her sincerity. What strings had she pulled to get in to the hospital to see me? Which favours had she called in? And with who? What extra suffering was in store for me because of it all? So, while we talked, my mind was whirring badly: "You'll never see her alive again after this visit" – that sort of thing. Usually, we'd sit and chat at one of the tables in the dining area. Sometimes, out of the blue, another patient would sit down with us. He or she would often just want to score a cigarette. I'd hand one over and we'd be left alone. It was rude, but those people didn't care. They didn't mean anything further by asking and, on balance, it was a small price to pay for some privacy.

Machine eye cigarettes

The smallest detail could totally rock my self-confidence. Even the way I extinguished my cigarette would be a solemn affair. If the cigarette then fell on the floor and kept on smoking, it was a sign that I was weak. Showing weakness was always a risk, you had to keep your guard up. It wasn't as serious as perhaps showing weakness in a full-on prison would be, but you still had to be careful. If I'd just finished smoking a cigarette out in the pod, and I'd thrown the butt just out of reach and it was still alight, I was trapped. So, I had another idea. I'd get control back by imagining the glowing, red tip of the cigarette was like a Terminator's eye. When that cigarette kept smoking just out of reach, I made myself keep watching it until it went out completely. I imagined it to be slowly losing power in front of me. Thinking I'd just watched a killer robot die made me feel a bit more in control of things.

Burning saucepan

In my flat, I wanted to kill myself. I went into several chemists asking for a big box of their strongest painkillers (only years afterwards did I learn that sleeping pills are what most people use – thank God they're controlled). Within the hour, I had loads of boxes with me. Then, I bought some brandy – so I'd go out in style. The next morning, I woke up on my kitchen floor - where I'd spent the night. There was a good amount of heat coming from the cooker. One of the empty pans had been burning all night and there was a fierce glowing red and smoke everywhere. I turned the cooker off and then heard the doorbell. It was my CPN, like we'd arranged. I'd forgotten he was coming, but was pleased to see him. I told him what I'd done and was quickly admitted to hospital.

Drinking water

Because I was bored, on the ward, I went through a phase of drinking water. I'd move about really considered and calm, slowly drinking water in front of anyone I saw. This doesn't sound that strange, but I was drinking from a bath foam bottle. I told everybody I saw in the hospital – doctors, patients, nurses, cleaners, workmen, my visitors - just why I was doing that. They'd ask me why I was drinking from a Radox bottle, which is what I wanted them to do, then, I'd tell them my story about how we judge each other. I had this little speech ready:

"Just because it's a bath foam bottle, it doesn't mean it has to have bath foam in it".

Then, they'd always ask:

"What if you get soap in your mouth?"

I'd tell them first: to relax. Then, I'd tell them that I'd thoroughly rinsed out the bottle before I drank from it. I'd even counted the number of times that I'd rinsed it out.

"How many times did you rinse it out?"

"I rinsed this bottle out twenty-two times before I put the water in it".

Never judge a book by its covers

I was so proud of myself at the time. There was no real chance at all of me drinking even a speck of bath foam by mistake. I explained this to everyone I encountered in the hospital. I remember thinking I'd won a major argument. I'd tell people:

"If this bottle had been the regular shape for a water bottle, you wouldn't think anything was wrong. Just because it's a different shape doesn't mean there's not the same drinking water inside it. It's the same with the people of the world. Just because someone looks evil, doesn't mean that they are evil. Never judge a book by its covers." Then, I'd smile knowingly and gently glide away. Of course, all this strange behaviour was addressed in ward round. Looking back, I think a fabric softener or a bleach bottle would've had even more of an impact – but I didn't have access to those at the time.

Scratching itches

Sometimes, I'd be daydreaming on my bed and I'd get an itch. Most people I guess would scratch it and hope it didn't return. But if I scratched an itch on the left side of my body with my right hand, the Universe would think I thought I was safe – I'd crossed the centre line. If I scratched an itch on my left side with my left hand, it showed I thought I was in danger because I *hadn't* crossed the centre line. Sometimes, I'd get an itch and not even bother scratching it at all. I was either too lazy to scratch it or I wasn't sure if I felt safe or not, or should I show I'm safe when I'm not? Also, while the itch is still there and I couldn't easily see the site of it, I'd imagine nasty reasons why it's still there. It must be an insect or a spider biting me! Then, I tell myself it's just paranoia. I realise you must be fairly lazy to just wish an itch away. In my experience (and if there's no real substance to the itch) the small patch of skin affected will revert to non-itchiness under its own volition.

Heir to the throne

I'd figured out that I was second in line for the English throne. My Dad had recently moved thousands of miles away to another country because that was where work had taken him. I thought I was the secret love child of Prince Charles and Camilla Parker-Bowles, before Prince William had been born. The Dad I knew had fled the country because he couldn't go on living a lie. I thought I'd been left, as a new-born baby, on my Mum's doorstep. Although I was always shown love, I thought she secretly felt inconvenienced by the whole thing because she was forced to care for me. Also, she was angry because she got no financial help from Buckingham Palace. I also thought that I'd said my first words when I was four years old (in reality, I'd started speaking at the age most children do, there was no silent protest from me after all). I saw it as more proof that, deep down, I was dumbfounded by what had happened. I didn't like all the hatred and lies. Another thing that helped me think all this royal worrying was true was that my Dad had been badly-affected by Princess Diana's death. Often when you strongly believe something, you'll make all the available evidence support your beliefs. In an ideal (perhaps unemotional) world, you'd build the body of evidence first and form your conclusions once you have all the facts.

Me, the nurse and our forbidden love

I was still in love with Gemma - a nurse who'd started working at the new hospital just after it opened. I knew she loved me back but I realised she had to put her job first and so couldn't start kissing me on the spot. My fantasy involved the two of us being brother and sister - both of us having been born to the same parents. These parents were still very much alive and well and living in Genoa, Italy (where Gemma and I had been separated at birth). The great prophecy foretold that once we became adults, we'd meet in a hospital, start a family together and rule the world in complete happiness.

Surface-to-air

This nurse escorted me to the garden and I was telling

her all about my worries. I thought my Mum's car mechanic had been gathering up powerful weapons. Pride of place in his garage was a surface-to-air missile launcher that he wanted to use to shoot down police helicopters. Right then, I thought I saw Gemma start crying. I figured she was upset because I was in such a crappy place mentally. She knew it'd take a long time for our happy, rule the world life to begin.

I offend a Mafioso

There I was, daydreaming in my flat and then the evil seeped in. A few times, this has made me try to kill myself. I used to smoke a great deal of weed in the past and that's why my head was so messed up. I was what's called "psychologically addicted" to cannabis and all of my flights of paranoid fancy stemmed ultimately from its use. So, I was just back from two weeks in Italy. I rarely go anywhere, maybe a day trip to Calais, but never anywhere by plane. So, it was a big deal for me. I was staying at a family friend's holiday home. There on my bed in the hospital, I began thinking about how I'd offended the house's owner. The story went that he was a Mafioso. Our friends had bought the house from the Mafioso and split it up into two smaller, luxury flats – one on the ground floor, one just above it. We were there to check the gas and electricity were in working order. Then, our friends could rent out the place knowing everything was working OK.

Contract out on my life

During the first week, I drank the half-dozen bottles of home-made wine in the upper flat where we were staying. I was relapsing badly by this point. After that, I secretly let myself in downstairs and drank all the wine in there, too. The old janitor who worked there had made this wine himself. It was a present from him to whomever was staying there. I thought that drinking another man's wine in Italy was like insulting his mother or something. Now I was back in the UK and the Italian Mafia knew I'd stolen all the wine from the downstairs flat. I knew this to be true. They were so angry that they were offering €10m to the man who successfully killed me. All this was designed to help the janitor regain his honour.

It's an Italian thing

I'd grown up knowing John. He lived just around the corner from my house. Importantly, I also knew he had an Italian-born parent. This Italian link was enough for him to first understand the offence and second come forward to claim the money. His national pride was so strong and he felt such pride for the old man that he even planned on giving the €10m fee to an Italian charity. As punishment for the theft of the wine in Italy, John was now coming to my flat to kill me. He'd never been to my flat before, but that was just a detail. Due to the resourcefulness of the Mafia, he'd found out exactly where I was living. Meanwhile, with all this whirring about in my head, I was feeling really depressed. Why had I decided to drink all the homemade wine from downstairs as well? I wanted to throw up, I felt so sorry. Then, I saw John in my mind walking along the street. He spoke to me:

"OK, fill the bath. Then turn off the taps. Undress and get in as usual. You will be my third kill. I can guarantee

that you will not make it through to the morning. I'm off
to Turks & Caicos after you're dead. Just so you know.
This, my friend - this is really not your night".

Bathing at gunpoint

I had him pictured in mind, with what I began calling a
"suicide screen." The tone of his voice was chilling and
you could tell he was just about keeping his temper. I
watched him walking down the street towards my house.
He was dressed appropriately for the cold, with black
gloves, big black coat and flat black hat. To show he
wasn't joking about killing me, he showed me the pistol
he had with him, then brought it back under his coat
again. After he'd told me to do that stuff with the bath,
the suicide screen faded away. It was about 10. 30pm by
this point. I followed his orders and got in the bath.
Then, the suicide screen appeared again. This time, he
spoke to me some more:

"OK then, mate. My killing you tonight is just a matter
of time. You really have only two choices. You either do
what I say, or you don't. You upset me? - I get to your
flat sooner. You do as I say? - I reach your flat a bit later
and you've bought yourself some time. I'm about a mile
away from your place right now. I'm giving you this
warning because we go back a fair way together. You
were a good bloke, in my eyes. Now you've gone and
ransacked another man's wine cellar. This isn't a
personal thing, it's an Italian thing. Now... Get out of the
bath".

After I heard this, I sheepishly got out of the bath.

I anger the hitman

"Now. Get back in again, and lay down fully in the water".

I did exactly what the man told me to. I saw John walking a bit slower, and I could breathe again. This was a good thing, I thought. A few more times I was made to get in the bath and lay down, and then get up and get out. I was feeling like a complete twat by now on a practical level. Then all the rigmarole started to make me angry. So, after his next command, I just ignored what he said – and stayed in the bath. I had visions of John starting to run.

"You're making me angry now. This is not a joke. Get out of the fucking bath!"

Defiant, now, I stayed lying down in the bath. I knew he was still coming, but I couldn't stand all the orders.

If I'm dead, he can't kill me

Then came the tipping point. I decided that if I was already dead when he arrived, he couldn't torture me while I was alive like he kept saying he would. In my kitchen, I still had access to a wide range of different medications. I thought I could kill myself by swallowing all of them. I gulped down all the pills I could find, followed by lots of booze. After that, I shut my eyes and waited to die. Next morning, I was still alive and even felt a bit better.

The female assassin

This good mood wasn't to last. The very next evening, I had another killer on my suicide screen. It was a girl this time, from martial arts class – a witness to my betrayal of the Chinese Mafia secret code. I'd secretly fancied her for a while, but I'd never told her. This time, my approaching assassin wasn't an Italian man with a gun, it was a sexy, well-trained girl. She'd been told how John had failed to kill me the night before. He'd been flown to Italy in shame. There was no partying in the Bahamas for him now. This gave me even more guilt to deal with, because I thought it was partly my fault.

Her bag full of weapons

Now, Samantha was coming to my flat - by motorbike, no less. She had a big rucksack on her back, filled with different tools. She told me she had these things with her:

- Sturdy handcuffs for restraint
- A towel bag for wetting and water-boarding
- Cable ties for tying left wrist to right ankle and vice versa
- A roll of duct tape for gagging
- A length of climbing rope for tying-up and strangling
- A plastic bag for asphyxiation
- A can of petrol and a lighter
- An axe for amputations and decapitation
- A big, sharp knife for blood-letting and stabbing
- A .357 Magnum revolver for shooting; and
- A lacy black negligee

Martial arts disruption

As you might think, I was interested to hear about the

negligee. I asked her about it as she sped towards me on her bike, weaving through the traffic. She said that she was already wearing it, and she planned to use it to seduce me. It was apparently how she preferred her killings. I couldn't argue. As for the other things in her bag, I didn't like the idea of those much. With this attempt on my life, she could drag my death out far longer than John had the night before. All the stuff she had with her meant that this time, my death would be much slower and much more painful. She'd been told to come and get me because of my rudeness in the martial arts class years before. Back there at the church hall, while I was psychotic, I'd pretty much signed my life away. Now, yet again, my suffering was mere hours away. How do you prepare to get laid, then tortured, and then killed? After we'd greeted one another like that mentally, a lot more give and take went on – like it had done the night before with the bath. The Chinese Mafia were trying to see how convinced I was that this girl was serious. Although I'd said I was sorry about disrupting the class years before, it seemed like nothing would wipe the slate clean. While she was on her way, my mood fluctuated wildly. I was shrugging off the threats one minute and petrified again the next.

The school for ninjas

There's more story to this martial arts girl coming for me. After I was thrown out of the martial arts class years before, I thought the classes there were a front for a ninja school. Oftentimes, people attending classes there would be called upon to kill people. As soon as I left after an evening of innocent, friendly martial arts, the others would each be headed for the airport. They'd be flying all over the world to kill whomever they had to kill – in reality, I had no contact with them outside of the class, how did I know if they flew about the world on business like this? Through unexplained, psychic connections, they'd listen out for the evening's code-word. Once they heard the teacher give the code-word, they could then go ahead with the kill. For security reasons, this code-word would be a different one every night. The thing was: I kept guessing this code-word. Then I'd think it repeatedly like a demented parrot. To everyone involved, it came across like I was trying to disrupt their subversive operations. I couldn't help myself from repeating (mentally) whichever word it was. This ridiculous breach of a confidence I hadn't even been given made the ninjas more furious with me with every night that passed.

Pirate suicide screen

The only other type of suicide screen I saw showed a very angry man. I could see his face in the darkness, with the tip of a hunting knife pointed up and resting just under his chin. He looked like some kind of pirate. It was much less personal than before, but still worrying. The first time I saw that pirate, I was scared again. At the time, he told me I was going to be forced to sign over all my money to him at knife-point and then he'd kill me.

Another breakdown

Soon enough, surrounded by all this mayhem, I was back in hospital. Here, I had access to well-trained nurses and doctors throughout the day and night. I told one of the nurses about my latest suicide screen and she said that it wasn't the first time she'd heard of the vision with the pirate and the knife. Some people do see that, but on balance it doesn't mean anything. She told me it was just a hallucination and that I should try not to worry. Since then, I've learned that the worry about something is usually worse than when the thing happens. For example, if you're worrying about exams, surgery or a driving test, it will probably turn out better than you thought it would. Worrying messes up the whole thing. If you try and think upbeat thoughts, it makes the waiting a bit easier to handle.

Suicide pills

For ages, I used to think there was a gap in the market for suicide pills for the public. In films and books, the spy would sometimes have a cyanide capsule with them. If they were going to be tortured and killed, they'd pop this pill and die without revealing anything too bad. If you went onto a psychiatric ward and offered cyanide pills to everyone, you'd be flooded with offers. If I'd seen cyanide on sale in my chemists, I would've bought and eaten one straight away. Now I'm out of that spiral, though, I'm glad these things are controlled. The same thing goes for guns. I've had serious mental problems for over a decade now. If I'd had a gun, and I was feeling hopeless, I think I would've blown my own head off years ago. Controlling dangerous things is very important - that's one of the reasons I'm still alive.

DJ appears in my room

In my flat daydreaming, a big-time radio DJ used to appear in my room. She was always angry, and a bit nosey, and she never came alone. She always had with her half a dozen heavily-armed Special Forces soldiers. They'd swarm up the stairs while I lay on my bed. Some would also swing in crashing through the windows. So, I lay there, minding my own business and she'd give the word to her troops. Without warning, they'd throw in smoke bombs and flashbangs and all the soldiers would move into my bedroom where I was in bed trying to rest. Once they'd "secured the flat" and settled down, they'd stand there like ghosts, guns raised at me in my bed. Sometimes during the raids, I'd try and retaliate, although I never actually got out of bed to do it. I'd try dreaming up soldiers of my own. This was really tiring and never really worked. On one occasion, I managed to summon up an older version of myself. This scared off the DJ and her soldiers for a while. I gave myself some much-needed advice and the timing was beautiful. I told myself not to worry and that everything would be OK. It was such a relief to hear a kind reassurance like that.

Loud music

While I was ill, I'd be really bolshie, but in a mainly normal way – like pushing the boundaries. What I mean is that I was too loud. There were times when I'd play music loudly in my flat in the summer. On my otherwise quiet estate I had all the windows and even the door wide open. I thought I was teaching all the neighbours and pedestrians what good music was. It got so bad that I was playing one band or DJ from one window, and a totally different band or DJ from another window.

Coughing on the train

I'd be sitting on a train headed in to central London and

I'd cough. Nothing unusual there. The only thing was that, at the time, there was another person in the carriage, too. And they'd cough. This was one-upmanship to me, so I coughed even louder than them. Usually, the other person didn't cough a second time. If they did cough again, I saw nothing wrong in just coughing again. This method of attack was great when a really stuck up woman or whatever would look at me or pass me and sniff. Straightaway, I'd sniff right back. I loved all that sort of thing at the time and it quickly cleared the seats around me! There was the time I was on a train and started laughing. I'd got a funny thought stuck in my head and couldn't shake it. It was rush hour when this happened but I saw no harm in just indulging myself laughing. I laughed so hard I fell off my seat and was rolling around in the aisles. Really, I was lucky not to get beaten up or arrested.

Dark but stylish movie poster

For a while, I had a very dark but stylish poster on my wall. It was one of the official ones from the film Godfather Part II. All the text was in Italian and in the middle there was a big picture of Al Pacino as Michael Corleone. I knew that film very well. He was sitting next to an urn which contained his father's ashes. There were three smaller pictures of (Tom Hagen – Robert Duvall, Fredo Corleone – John Cazale and Kay Adams – Diane Keaton) along the bottom, and another one of Robert De Niro (as a young Vito Corleone) with his family present at the top. I used to get stoned and gaze into that poster quite a lot. Soon enough, I didn't even need to get stoned for it to bother me. I'd stare at it and see the killer Michael's fingers twitch now and then – subtle commands to: kill him, kill her, move on him. It was only after several uncomfortable years that I finally passed it on. I used to think "it's just a poster, what's wrong with me?" But, more importantly, I've learned that some things are just more dangerous than others. That poster featured a fiercely negative set of images and eventually I learned not to stare at it for long periods at a time.

Shaved head relapse

So, I was admitted to the hospital with a totally bald, shaved head. When I'd gone into the hairdressers to have it done, the lady asked me about three or four times if I was totally sure I wanted to be shaved: a "zero all over". I had no clippers of my own, so I kept on at her. Soon enough, all my lovely hair was on the floor. She'd done a great job – taking it as close to the skin as she could get. With my new look that summer, on buses and trains, I could feel people thinking about me, judging me. I looked like a neo-Nazi, a racist thug. It was stupid. I started worrying so much that I ended up back in hospital, mainly because of the skinhead haircut. During the stay that time, I managed to always have a bag of fresh spinach with me. I'd read somewhere that if you eat plenty of spinach, it helps your hair to grow. I really wanted my hair back. I've shaved my head fully three times during my life. Although I look OK bald, I prefer having hair on my head. I really didn't like the dirty looks I kept getting.

Superstitious New Age girl

One patient I met in hospital was a short, New Age girl. She was very superstitious. When she was given her meds at the meds hatch, she'd start casting spells on them. She'd wave her hands all over the pills and hum a little tune quietly before she took them from the nurse. I even saw her spin around on the spot twice before answering the phone. Whenever she caught a tiny money spider, she'd take the thread with the spider on the end and swing it gently around her head in a slow, whirling action. She'd then leave the spider to its own devices somewhere on her hair –which I thought was a bit risky. Still, this spell was designed to bring her more money. When I asked her about what she did, she became deadly serious. She was convinced the universe would fast-track her to fortune if she upheld all these beliefs.

Mane / nocte

At home, cooking was a luxury. In hospital, people made toast, heated up porridge in the microwave or made Pot Noodles – but that was it. While you were on Overnight Leave, you could fry bacon and eggs for a sandwich, anything you liked. Another good thing about being away overnight on leave was that you could take your meds whenever you liked. In hospital, it was strict: eight in the morning for *mane* meds and ten in the evening for *nocte* meds. When I was back home again in my flat, I took my meds just before bed and then just out of bed the next day. In these very small ways, I'd start to feel like I was back in charge of my life again.

Demon controls the body's insides

While in hospital, I thought the demonic creature I'm about to discuss was my Mum. Whenever I saw it, while I was unwell, I always thought of how evil it was. I couldn't get my head around why it was so cruel, using its powers to hurt all the other animals on earth. The Geographer had given it powers over all the creatures on the earth – notably their insides. If a person disrespected it, it'd retaliate swiftly and with deadly force. At the very best, one of its spells would cause someone to have indigestion. At the worst, it'd bestow upon someone a heart attack, a stroke or (in women) a miscarriage.

Mum possessed

That demon would walk into the dining area with cigarettes for me as usual and, inside, I'd be shocked again. Up 'til that visit, I'd thought the Pope, the Queen, or someone else really powerful had had this demon killed for being plain evil. Every time I saw it (during this time), I was always wondering how it'd bought them off. How was it even still alive? I really thought that while I was in hospital, this creature felt happy and safe. It could use the fact that I was locked up in there to its benefit. People would pity it while it played the victim. Each time when it left the hospital, I had to try and make sense of my thoughts again – until they were capsized all over again.

The slaying method

Assuming my Mum and brother were two demons, I helpfully then became aware of how to finish them off. For each there was a totally unique method to follow. The steps had to be followed to the letter if you wanted to rid the earth of whichever demon it was. If even one mistake was made, it could rear up even more powerfully. What follows is like a handbook for how to kill them.

Corpse swells up

To kill the first one, it would need to be killed like a normal human first. Bearing in mind this whole thing is from my paranoia, a single gunshot to the head is fast. So, this demon would be shot and killed, ideally in daylight in wasteland miles from anywhere. Shooting it fatally is just the beginning - now, things get strange. A putrid smell of rotting flesh will immediately emanate from the corpse laying on the grass. The body will turn a dark green and black colour and then it'll start to swell up in size. It will swell and swell until it's grown to the size of a camper van. Once it's reached this size, it'll stop growing but the smell will be worse than ever.

Cut into the flesh

Left in this state, the huge lump of rotting flesh will stay like this for about a week. After that time, it will shrink back down until it looks like a normal human corpse again. Then, the demon will get up off the floor and walk away – ready to get back to punishing the innocent. If you wanted to finish it off – for the good of Mankind – there were steps you had to take. With the demon still swollen up, you had to get a sharp knife and slice right into it. This would let off a loud, hellish screaming, but you'd be safe from any real danger. You had to be sure you carved deep into that stinking flesh, right through to the middle.

Ignore the screaming

Amidst the smell and everything else inside the big, slimy demon mass, you'd have to find a ball in there –

this represents its life force. You should then remove this ball. Once you get this out, you carefully must break it open. You can do this on hard earth, or against a rock. This will reveal a smaller ball inside the first. This second, smaller ball is very important, if you messed up any of these stages, the creature would live forever. Once you had hold of that second ball, you had to plunge it deep into the screaming demon flesh. It had to be left inside the demon, roughly where you found the first ball. Once the smaller ball is put firmly inside the thing again, the giant wound will seal up. Then, the screaming will stop. Then, for a couple of seconds: absolute silence.

Ignore the persuasion

Once the huge gash has finished closing, you're on to the last stage of the killing. The flesh will keep closing in on itself and in on itself until a tiny, but powerful, black hole appears. This will be floating just a few feet above the ground. When you see this, you should stand way back. For the next half an hour or so, this mini black hole will powerfully try to suck into it everything nearby. Its range here is about thirty feet. The demon, having realised that it's really dying, will be trying to suck people in to it. It will try and tempt people to follow it down into hell – and some will go. In a beautiful, golden voice, it'll say things like:

"Let me bring you and your family untold riches," or claims like

"Come with me and never again feel pain," or

"Follow me into eternal paradise."

It'd promise these things to anyone passing by. None of it would be true, of course. When that half an hour of promises is up, the black hole will close and there'll be nothing left. Every living soul on the earth-plane will instantly feel generally much better. By killing this demon, you will have banished to hell a pivotal, powerful and malevolent force.

Demon controls the body's surfaces

The second demon (embodied by my brother) had domain over the *surfaces* of all of God's creatures - the hair, the skin and the nails. As with the first demon, because of its powers, it had countless fans, friends, and followers. Whimsically, it could curse someone, or an animal, with a fatal illness. Similarly, as a way of punishing disloyalty or as a show of strength, it could curse someone with a skin disease, hair loss, deafness; things like that. It was respected because it used its powers in these ways and because of the powers, it was feared.

Racism

Racism was rife throughout the world and hatred had become a common thing. Hatred had become something to aspire to. This demon could also deaden its own skin or change the colour of its eyes whenever it wanted. This meant it could skinny dip in frozen lakes. It could drink boiling hot coffee or soup in one go. It could also control when it climaxed and have sex for ages – if it so chose. Also, it could shape-shift at will, causing its eyes to go slit (like a cat's) on command and cause its teeth to look fierce.

Hole in the ground

To kill this second, terrible demon, you had to first kill it like a human - with a gun is best. Shooting it from 200 yards away was optimum. 200 yards was the radius of its immediate death-throes. Once you'd killed it, you had to be standing well clear. Once the official life force had left its body, a hole would open exactly beneath where it fell. Here, a mini volcano will appear. This will start spewing up and throwing out liquid rock and fire. Now, the killer (and only the killer), using their imagination, had to cause the demon's life force to diminish. While the portal was open, the killer had to spawn many different animals. The creation of each one will drain the hellish life force of the demon, one animal at a time. These animals would then appear from the hole and run or fly away from it, as regular animals would.

Ten of each animal

So, as the killer thought of the next animal to be created, that animal would appear from out of the volcanic hole and run away. If the killer thought of a hippo, a hippo would appear, and run away. If the killer thought of a panda, a tiger or an eagle, they would each appear from out of the hole and run or fly away. Also, if they successfully spawned an elephant, because of its mass, it'd cause a larger diminishing of energy than of, say, a spider. On top of that, the rules stated that the killer could only cause the spawning of the same species of animal or bird ten times. After ten kangaroos etc. he/she'd be obliged to consider maybe ten lions or ten rhinos. This meant the killer had to have a fair knowledge of the animal kingdom. If he/she kept thinking of different animals, the demon's volcanic energy would be steadily drained. And as that energy was spawning every new animal, slowly but surely, the demon's overall life force was caused to diminish. With enough grit, patience and knowledge of different animals, the energy of the demon will be exhausted.

Flame-covered figure

A secondary problem caused by this killing method was that the animals really had nowhere to go after they'd been created from out of the hole. As soon as they appeared they'd run off at a random direction and cause chaos in the vicinity. After about half an hour of this, the demon in human form would eventually climb up himself and crawl out from the hole. This demon figure would be made head to toe from fire. It was like a scene from out of a horror film, but no joke if you were too close. This flame-covered figure would then very slowly walk about – it wouldn't be moving quickly because lots of its energy would've had to have gone into all the animals. This figure can also *throw* fire at people it comes across, with a range of about ten feet. Often, when people see this flame-covered demon, they freeze - rooted to the spot with fear. The molten flames figure then either throws fire at them or approaches them and touches them with its fiery hands. The victims then die screaming from the burns.

Residual wildlife

After the dust clears, humankind will again be safe. The demon will have exhausted all its energy and returned down to hell. After a while, the molten rock will cool and the hole will seal up. As for all the spawned animals, they'll have dispersed into the immediate environment. Since they were in no way supernatural, before long, they'd get tired, hungry and confused. Some will've been in car accidents, some adopted by strangers, but most captured by the authorities and taken to zoos. As for the rest, as days pass, they'll become emaciated and die from hunger. Immediately following the death of this demon, every living soul on the earth-plane will feel an unexplained lift in ambient mood.

Demon controls twisted cables

The third and final demon I thought had possessed my girlfriend. It oversaw tangled cables and doled out everlasting rape in its realm of hell. Whenever I saw messy, tangled cables, I'd think of this demon. I thought that, apart from just being lazy, the reason most people didn't sort their tangles out was because they were trying to avoid the negative consequences. So, if someone undid a tangle - they'd be raped; if they left it knotted - they'd be OK. This must be why the patients' phone was always so badly tangled, I figured to myself. The lead joining the handle with the main part of the phone was always all twisted up. I hated having to see it like that, but I didn't have the guts to straighten it out. Or, more likely, I didn't want to jeopardise my own safety.

Killer beetles

To kill this tangle demon, as with the other two, the specifics were exhaustive. You had to be careful. Only a distant kill (like a shooting or a bomb) was gonna do it this time – although you had to be within about 200 yards, or underwater. The main thing to remember was that again, once you'd killed it, you had to act fast. In fact, the killer was in danger straightaway. He or she really had to be ready. Straight after being initially killed, the demon's body from the chest down would explode into hundreds of tiny beetles. These beetles were angry and blood-thirsty – and they were out to get their master's killer. The only way to escape the little, killer insects was to kill the main demon underwater, because then they couldn't breathe. Also, if you could outrun them, you could dive into water yourself to get away from them. The beetles, with their razor-sharp teeth, would then drown and you'd walk off OK. And, of course, after the tangle demon had been killed, souls the world over would rest slightly easier for a reason they can't explain.

Vampire baths

At my flat in south east London, I started taking long baths. It just felt like the right thing to do. They could easily take 2 hours - sometimes longer. For the long, long ones, I got some old jeans and put them underwater by my head end, just under my back. I would top up the bathwater with more hot water every half hour or so during these marathon baths. Sometimes I'd read, sometimes I'd listen to music. Usually, though, I just spoke to myself. My favourite thing was to speak like Dracula. Every "r" would be heavily-rolled. At the time, I was pretending I was a cat. My monologues always started like this:

"Ammm cat. Enjoy eatingg birrrd, and mouse. You give me warrrm place to rest? Ammm cat. I brrring mouse forrr you".

"I brrring you morrre mouse than you cann eat. I brrring you frrresh birrrd for brrreakfast".

"Ammm cat. Ammm wet. Ammm wet cat".

Strippers by the light switches

Then, a thought dawned on me. No-one from my housing association had ever checked up on me for the whole ten years I'd been renting. This wasn't surprising, I'd been a good tenant. And as far as I knew, there'd been no complaints made about me. So, I took it to mean I could do whatever I wanted with the flat's interior. Why not? No-one would come 'round and stop me. I went straight to all my old porn magazines. I set about cutting out photos of my favourite stripper girls from the magazines and put them up on the walls. I was careful not to put up actual porn – I didn't want to look sleazy. I only put up the photos of the girls in the magazines *before* they'd stripped off. See normally, the photo shoots in porn magazines are like a sort of striptease. You turn the pages, and (in the photos) the clothes gradually are removed. I put up all these photos next to and around the light-switches in the flat, so I'd always notice them. At the time, I had a mental friendship with each of the girls. I thought I was being so clever with my "still-clothed" approach. I thought it was only me who knew they were proper exhibitionists. At the time, I was proud to know all those sexy, stripper girls (that I'd certainly never met) on the walls.

Black spray paint

Just after I'd peppered all around my light switches with fully-clothed, female strippers, I bought a big can of black, Audi spray paint. At the time, the floors throughout the flat were all black. I was depressed and sad most of the time probably due, in part, to that fact. Anyway, I started spraying the paint all over the walls.

After a while of wanting to spray something important, I thought I'd spray Greek letters – mainly the "λ - lambda" letter. I knew that in America the universities have clubs for students, the names of which comprise Greek letters, like Phi Beta Kappa. I thought I'd start my own – Lambda Lambda Lambda (λλλ). For ages, I thought I was a trailblazer, but it turns out there is actually a fraternity called λλλ.

High off the fumes

Sadly, while I was spraying black symbols all over the walls, I'd forgotten to open any windows. And, with no ventilation, the concentrated paint fumes meant that I really couldn't sleep. Every time I closed my eyes, I was forced to hallucinate. I'd have a busy TV screen in my mind that I was forced to watch. It soon became annoying. As far as I can remember, the images were of old TV adverts I'd seen years before. While all these events had led to another breakdown for me, my poor brother and family had to clean up the mess. I never set out to hurt anyone, but it looks like I kept smoking weed to do just that. I'm a stubborn person, though, and sadly, it's taken many years for me to receive this message. It's embarrassing and disheartening looking back now and the general situation never comes up. I think now that it's best to try and learn from the painful times and move on better prepared with the knowledge you've gained.

Man vs. wok

In my flat while I was watching the TV for real, I was feeling very lazy. In the lounge, I started dropping my cigarette ash directly onto the floor. I sat there doing that while I drank my way through my nightly six-pack of lager. Then, (the now late) Brian Sewell came on the screen. I'd always hated his posh, supercilious voice. I thought there was nothing else for it, I had to stand up for the common man! I went into the kitchen and got myself an old wok. I took it into my bare-floored, black, ashy lounge and I whacked that thing on the floor over and over as hard as I could. Whenever he opened his mouth to speak – another whack. I really thought that, through the TV screen, he could somehow feel that I had a problem with him. I whacked that poor wok on the floor repeatedly until it was just a blob of black metal with a wooden handle. It was a metal blob that had become warm to the touch because of the energy going through it. I really thought I'd taught Brian Sewell a lesson that night.

Medieval sounds

Sometimes, I'd go medieval. At random times of the night, I'd let various metal items like cutlery and tools clatter onto the floor. I imagined I was living in the era of knights and swords and suits of armour. I was recreating the sorts of noises people in those big, draughty castles would have heard as they lived in olden times. I threw things at the walls. I threw things at the floor. After a few nights of this, I remembered I had neighbours to the side and underneath me, too. They were understanding and accepted my apologies. Thankfully for me, even after a week or two of my dark-ages noises, they still forgave me.

I break my swords

A few months previous, I'd gone to Edinburgh for the

annual comedy festival. Randomly, I found a martial arts shop that sold fancy, Japanese swords in threes on display in the window. The swords had green scabbards and were mounted on a dark wood stand. I went inside and bought a set. As soon as I got the swords back to my flat, I put them on my TV. These swords were the holy grail of medieval clanging and so were my next weapon of choice. I really was raising hell in that flat. The same night I battered the wok, I went just outside in the night and began hitting those swords on the concrete with all my might. One by one, I bent each of them totally out of shape. Sometimes, the swords would still be in their scabbards, I didn't care. I still smashed them apart on the floor. Looking back, it was about me venting my anger. As far as I could see, I was the only person for miles around who was truly alive. Frankly, I'm just glad no-one nearby beat me up or had me arrested.

Nunchuks go missing

I had a great pair of nunchuks (Bruce Lee style rice flails) that a friend of the family had given me a long while before. They were pale wood with fancy stones and carvings on them. They had ball-bearings on both ends of the linking chain which meant no tangles when you spun them. I wanted some weapons ready outside my door, in case I was attacked while trying to get back in. I really had no enemies. Still, I hid the nunchuks in amongst some plants by my front door. Months and months went by and I hadn't been attacked. About a year later, I looked for them, but they were gone. Probably just as well, really. I had no skill with them. If I had been attacked, the other person would've more likely taken them off me and hit me over the head with them.

Bugged by the president

My flat was near a big factory. Now and then, the TV would click, even when switched off (this is actually because of the temperature changes causing expansion and contraction within the structure). The TV was haunted. Furthermore, it was proof that George W Bush (president at the time) had put a bugging device in it to keep me under surveillance. Why him? I figured that the factory was owned by an American corporation, so the American president would have access to it. I thought that the American factory and its grounds qualified it to be officially American soil, much like international embassies abroad. My TV remote control would also click. This was yet another bug hidden and intended to keep me under greater surveillance. If ever I looked casually out the window, I was reminded I was in the crosshairs of a US sniper laying on the factory's roof. Then, I'd immediately close the curtains and hide.

G&T leads to relapse

So, I'd just been admitted to a crisis centre (B&B) for the mentally ill and aside from where I'd found myself, things seemed fine. There was a pub five minutes' walk away. I went there alone and ordered a gin and tonic – not my usual drink to begin with. I wasn't used to the gin or the tonic. It was so sour that I only took a tiny sip every now and then. This was very out of character for me. I was sitting in the beer garden alone with my drink in the sun. I made that one G&T last the whole hour I was there. Afterwards, I returned to the B&B but I was acting strangely then. Volvo cars at the time were marketing their "Side Impact Protection System" which

were essentially airbags for the sides as well as the front.
I found myself fixated with this SIPS technology,
especially how the acronym read as just letters. If
anyone asked me how much I'd had to drink, I repeated
the same phrase every time: "SIPS. Just SIPS". I was
acting distracted and very, very quiet in speech. I don't
think they understood the Volvo connection - I'm not
really even sure if I did.

Side Impact Protection System

I thought I was being clever and that they'd appreciate
my ingenuity, but I wasn't saying anything else. Time
after time, I'd answer with the same phrase, I knew that
I'd only taken sips of that gin and tonic in the pub. I was
trying to convey to them I'd had a safe amount of alcohol,
if only I'd rephrased it! Before long, I was being
informally interviewed. I was sat in the room and we
talked, but SIPS was all I whispered. Then, the staff
member left the room for a while. In about fifteen
minutes time, the whole SIPS fiasco had led to me being
guided into a cab headed for the hospital, where I was to
begin yet another spell of residential care. So, the SIPS
fiasco played out at the B&B. The place was run by the
same NHS trust as the hospitals. It was intended to be a
stepping stone for the patients before returning home.
There were also two rooms called "crisis" and "respite".
Perhaps because they were next to one another, it took
me ages to think about how each was different from the
other. The ban on smoking inside in public spaces came
into effect on July 1st, 2007, of course. Not everyone
smoked, but if you did smoke, there was a room in the
warm with a TV where you could do that.

Great food at the B&B

The food at the B&B was fantastic. Every patient staying there had round-the-clock access to a big fridge full of food. There were always yoghurts, cakes, pies, cold cuts, soft drinks, milk and juice, all readily available. It was much better than what I had in my own fridge at home. Whenever my stay there finished and I left to go home, I always found that I'd put on a bit of weight. The formal mealtimes were also brilliant there. There was a full-time cook who'd prepare delicious meals for us every evening. Breakfast was also great –this was my favourite meal. Every morning, there would appear huge, separate serving bins. There'd be a breakfast buffet including: scrambled eggs, bacon, sausages, mushrooms, hash browns, bubble and squeak, beans and toast - everything. If you got along with the other people, life could be OK there.

Great staff at the B&B

All of us staying at that B&B facility were each given a key to the building – another way they helped build trust. One time, I wanted to shake a hanger-on after I'd been out late drinking. Instead of using my key, I knocked on the main door instead. One of the nurses opened the door to me and the girl disappeared. There was also the time where I'd gotten a cab to the other side of London by mistake. Again, the nurse sympathised, spoke to the cabbie for me and even paid the extra cab fare the driver was demanding. Then, the nurse let me pay him back when I could afford to.

I really should've brushed my teeth

So, I was in my flat and I was having a really bad time of it dentally. In the space of a week, two of my teeth cracked and crumbled away. The first tooth broke after I drank a can of full-sugar Coke – and that night didn't brush my teeth. The next day, with the sugar from the Coke still in my mouth, I was eating toast. Then, I discovered I was eating something much crunchier than toast. I was shocked. I was crunching a bit of my tooth that had broken away. I totally blame the sugar in the Coke. It was thoughtless of me to drink that and not brush afterwards. Later the same week, I was drinking full-sugar Coke again. The next day, again after not brushing, I found myself opening a bottle of red wine – another big no-no, in fact. It was a twist top bottle, and I used my mouth to open it, as I always did. While I was doing that, part of another tooth broke off in my mouth. Since I sometimes over-think things and get worried, I feared the worst. I made the links that only a paranoid man can. For me, it was a warning from Jesus Christ. He was telling me to change my ways. The losses of the teeth were linked to Jesus because of His Body (bread, toasted or otherwise) and His Blood (red wine). I felt wretched after that, not to mention that I now had a slightly altered smile.

I observe my visitor

When I was admitted to the closed hospital for the first time, Sara came in to visit me. Four things struck me about her visit. First, she understood how sorry I was. Second, she returned to me a small pouch of tobacco I'd left at the class that night months before. Third, she asked me why I hadn't just run off after having smashed the pub's windows in town. And fourth, her behaviour as she waited for me in the visitor's room. It was quite a small thing and I didn't even bring it up at all. As she was waiting, I watched her briefly through a window. Whenever anyone looked through and tried to scare her with an angry, "mental patient" face, she just dusted off her shoulders. This was way before you see some rappers do it now in videos. That dusting-off was as if to say:

"I don't care what you think of me. I'm still here. Still holding things down".

People denied entry

I felt like a sitting duck in the open hospital. I was still dwelling on my actions in that martial arts class years before. I thought Sara was coming to get me. If I gave them her name, the staff could block her at the intercom. I was certain she was coming to kill me. I'd broken an unwritten, Chinese Mafia rule that demands respect for the teacher always. Those rules were thousands of years old. She was also bringing Scott. It didn't matter that I'd apologised, or even that the two of them had accepted my apologies. While I was with the nurse jotting down these two names, I put some other people on that list as well. I was worrying also about Jack Nicholson and Robert De Niro. They were also coming to get me. Every patient in the hospital had a list of people they wanted barred from the hospital.

Bloodthirsty movie stars

I'd been worried about Nicholson and De Niro before. I could see them landing on a small, private airstrip in northern Scotland so they'd avoid the paparazzi. I saw them then driving all the way south to meet me – to kill me in my bed if need be. I was really scared. This attack was as inevitable as dawn - like the attack from the two martial artists. Soon, they'd start torturing me with pliers and acid and electricity and all sorts. Whenever I heard his voice in my head, Jack Nicholson (as his character from The Witches of Eastwick or The Shining) always called me "princess," which sounded about right. Robert De Niro (present as his violent Goodfellas character) was always angry full stop - just because I was alive at all. The two of them had been working for The Geographer for their whole lives. On top of these four people, I also added Al Pacino to this list. I included him because I thought he was a bona fide boss in the Mafia – thanks to his roles in Scarface and the Godfather films. I still had glitter-bugged rooms to deal with and Al Pacino was a serious threat through my belief system with those.

Staff get star struck

So, Nicholson and De Niro were speeding south towards me from Scotland. Pacino was psychically coordinating everything and I was trapped in the hospital and prevented from leaving. I was a sitting duck. Apart from banning them from coming into the hospital, I told no-one else. In fact, straight after I'd told the nurses, they'd talked to the celebrities, taken payoffs and had hiked up my evening meds without telling me. I thought that when they reached the hospital, the nurses would ask for autographs and photos (instead of protecting me) with the two actors. They'd charm the nurses, get access to my bedroom while I slept, gag me and put a sack over my head. The nurses would have scaled up my sedatives so the abduction would go even more smoothly. That very night, I was to be taken to a remote, dark cave and my life being tortured would begin. I started thinking how I could protect my hospital, my hospital room, and my hospital bed. I imagined massive spikes ready to skewer intruders and Indiana Jones style booby-traps designed to kill or disable. Sadly, these defences relied on me being conscious for them to be effective. This was why I couldn't afford to fall asleep. The two martial arts teachers were also bearing down on me, independently of the three actors.

TYPICAL LEVELS OF LEAVE FROM THE OPEN HOSPITAL

#1 - Escorted leave to the garden

Here, I'm describing here every increment of leave I can think of - between being first admitted and finally discharged. Each amount of leave was usually the same amount per day. The first level of leave from the hospital was Escorted Leave to the Garden. This meant a nurse took you to a walled garden. During this trip, what you said and did was carefully observed. If you behaved well, this would count in your favour. The garden was about the size of a tennis court. Most of the nurses were chatty and the time (anything up to thirty minutes) passed easily. It was a great relief to get outside in the fresh air, especially so if was your first time using this leave. The nurse would tell you to get a drink and bring your smokes. Then, they ushered you downstairs and along some corridors. In the garden, there was a wooden hut with some seats inside it. Also, there were ashtrays and a green, plastic table. At the far end of the garden was a shed, where the garden tools were kept safely under lock and key. If you had family/ friends visiting, they could also act as your escort. As a side note, your leave would often remain the same until the next weekly wardround. Outside of wardrounds, a nurse could sometimes withdraw your leave as a punishment.

#2 - Unescorted leave to the garden

Unescorted Leave to the Garden was the next increment of leave the doctor could grant. It meant that you could go to the garden by yourself. Being alone for a little while was a great change from the day to day tensions. Sometimes, there'd be another patient in the garden, but usually you were alone. When asking for extra leave and discharge, your prime concern had to be the nurses' trust. Nurses were the eyes and ears of the doctors. If they believed you wanted to heal, this would be strongly encouraged. Some people who were given Unescorted Leave to the Garden had jumped over the fence and run off. But the police soon caught them and brought them back. Once back at the hospital, that patient had his leave completely reset, which meant he had to rely on friends and other patients to bring him things.

Handover

In between the half hour ward rounds throughout the week the nurses would discuss all the patients. Any important incidences would be brought up at these meetings. As different shifts of nurses arrived and left, there was always purposely a slight overlap. This regular, hour-long, overlap meeting was called Handover. Handover was always a headache for the patients. While handover was underway, there was usually only one nurse sitting outside the control room. They couldn't leave their posts. It wasn't that we didn't like what they were saying about us during handover, we just didn't like having to wait – there was enough of that already. As patients, we always seemed to become more demanding while handover was happening. There'd be all the usual questions, most demands would often be to just test the staff and create a little anarchy:

- Can we have more milk in the kitchen?
- Can I have that other pack of cigarettes my Mum left me?

- Can we have the menus for takeaway deliveries? Where's my phone charger?
- Can we have another ball for the ping pong table?
- Is my lawyer here yet?
- This treatment is against my human rights!

#3 - Escorted leave to the Grounds

The next increment of leave was Escorted Leave to the Grounds. Again, they'd only give you this after you'd waited for another whole week, showing good patience, rage control and general compliance with staff. Even so, it was another step towards full discharge, and it was almost always a welcome development for the patient. Escorted Leave to the Grounds from the hospital was great news, more so if you'd been waiting a while to get it. If you were lucky, you'd have a pretty nurse going with you. This type of leave was the next increment up from Garden Leave. This leave didn't reach as far as the tobacco shops in the High Street, but there was the sweet shop and the main hospital restaurant to go to. The sweet shop didn't sell tobacco, but it sold something better: Campino strawberry boiled sweets. They were delicious, and also quite high in sugar. So, with the pretty escort and my sweets, we'd go to the main hospital restaurant.

#4 - Unescorted leave to the grounds

The next increment of leave was Unescorted Leave to the Grounds. You could spend forever on the benches in the sun outside the restaurant. Also, you didn't have to buy up loads of packs of Campino sweets. Some patients, when given Leave to the Grounds, would head straight off the grounds and right into the town centre, which was strictly speaking not allowed. Town was a good fifteen minutes away on foot. This walking would easily eat into your total time off the ward. If you were desperate to get there, it was possible to catch a bus. When it came time to use your leave, it was a thrill even deciding with the nurses when you'd return. Unlike life in the closed hospital, which was stricter, the nurses didn't jot down what you were wearing whenever you left. Also, there was more discretion regarding times shown by the nurses on duty. I heard of one man catching a train to London Bridge (going AWOL from the hospital) where he found a public internet café. He then found his friends online, got the details of a party, and travelled all the way to Brighton where he partied 'til the following day. After that, he turned himself in and returned to the ward.

Proud to have breakfast

Generally, you'd be given about thirty or forty minutes from when you left the hospital. This meant you had time for a meal at the restaurant (which has sadly since closed down). If you arrived early enough, the breakfast buffet items were still all there on hot-plates. They would've been waiting there all morning, but for someone fresh out of the hospital for a while, it was like heaven. The main thing was that it was a meal *for me –* and *paid for by me*. Also, it was in a place used by the other hospital staff. It helped me to feel I was slightly more normal – I could have been anyone. After that, I'd enjoy a cigarette or two just outside in the sun.

#5 - Escorted leave to the shops

If you were lucky enough to have plenty of visitors, they would each act as your escorts. If you had fallen out with everyone you knew, you were out of luck. Obviously, the doctor would tailor the conditions of his leave awards depending on the individual's circumstances. If you needed a nurse for your leave and there were none free, it would often be another week of waiting. Equally, it could really feel euphoric. You'd emerge from a ward round where, not two minutes ago you'd been given the next increment of valuable leave *usually, the meeting would take about twenty minutes. There'd be discussions, OT second opinions, ward nurses offering observations of behaviour and compliance with medication. The awarding of leave to the patient often came right at the end – because behaviour during the ward round also factored in the decision. Doctor: "OK then, I think we can safely extend your leave to Escorted Leave to the Shops, for *glances at a nurse who acts agreeable* two hours?" Then, I'm about to burst, I'm so happy. "OK, then, I'll see you next week!" Then he folds shut his dossier on me and I'm beckoned to the door with my care coordinator.* Endorphins would come rushing as you asked your care co-ordinator if that *was actually decided*. At this precise point in time, you know better than the nurses. The rooms where ward round happens and the nurse control centre are both at different ends of the building. You'd approach a nurse in the control room and tell them with relish "I'm going to the town with my friend - I just got Unescorted Leave to the Shops." When they hear this, they must authenticate your claim - anyone could walk in and tell them that. Then, there would follow some to-ing and fro-ing by the nurses checking your claim. Finally, it would be decided that the doctors had in fact rubber-stamped the leave you claimed. And with everyone's blessing, you got to take that day's leave right then.

#6 - Unescorted leave to the shops

If this was your leave status, you could go pretty much anywhere alone. Usually, you had about four hours off the ward. If you arranged to take your daily leave at around the same time as another patient, it wasn't unusual for you to meet up again at a nearby pub maybe and have a few beers. If the two of you staggered leaving the ward slightly, like maybe ten minutes apart, this helped disguise your plans. If you covered your alcohol breath with mints just before you returned, the staff would never catch on. After that, you'd meet later in the smoking room as usual. For us patients, we felt like pirates!

Running errands for ward-bound patients

As the distances and times of your leave increased, you could still spend your time at the other places, too. If you were allowed to the town, you could still go just to the garden, if that's all you wanted to do. Also, if you had leave to the shops in town, nobody was forcing you to go there. If you had Leave to the Shops, it was usual that you get hold of some creature comforts like tobacco and junk food for other patients, whose movements would be more restricted than yours.

Be kind to strangers

Sometimes, I've even been trusted with a fellow patient's bank card and PIN number ("I want you to go to the bank machine and withdraw £50. Spend £30 on tobacco, you know what I smoke, £15 on Dairy Milk fruit and nut, and you can keep the change" sort of thing). Patients you'd met maybe just the day before would have this much faith in you. It either meant that they properly considered you trustworthy or that they really didn't have a clue. A large percentage of the people in the hospital already lived in the grey areas of the law. I've no idea what the punishment was for stealing someone's bank card, but I've got a feeling it would've been messy *these were often people who managed to embrace their illness in their daily lives somehow. One time, we were all sitting in the smoking room listening while one of the ladies coordinated an attack on a convicted "kiddie-fiddler". He'd served his time and had just been released. This lady was now making and taking calls left and right so this man was trapped somewhere and beaten shitless. This was apparently the street justice her whole estate felt he deserved. "He'll be at the Moon and Sun pub from five onwards." "Get him to stay there, I don't care what it takes!" "Ok, we've gotta get him into the carpark. You know what to do." With that, she defiantly snapped shut her oyster phone. A few hours later, she fills us in on the man's condition. "We got him good. *laughs* He'll never have children now, his bollocks are the size of pumpkins. He's black and fuckin' blue all over. The little cunt." They say "Hell hath no fury like a woman scorned?" You'll hear no argument from me.* If you hadn't misused your leave and were generally calm and compliant, you were in with a good chance of more leave. The nurses and doctor would discuss your progress in handover that day, and then in ward round the following week. Of course, if you broke that trust, your leave would be cut or they'd just withdraw it all.

#7 - Overnight leave

Once I'd earned it, I'd be given Overnight Leave. If it was Escorted, I'd need a visitor to go with me. If it was Unescorted, I could be alone for that evening and just lounge around the flat. I could smoke, drink and order takeaways – relishing the freedoms I couldn't enjoy in hospital. Just before leaving the hospital, you had to get your TTOs (stands for To Take Out – essentially, all the meds you're prescribed for the time you'll be spending off the ward). Sometimes, I wouldn't tell anyone else I was going away on leave. I felt like a right, little celebrity waiting there in the smoking room with the others. Soon enough, a nurse would appear and tell me my TTOs were ready. When they said that, I'd take them and walk grandly out of the room, dispensing hurried goodbyes like a rock star.

#8 - Week-long leave

The very last type of leave to be given, before a complete discharge, was Week-Long Leave. If I'd had the ward round on a Wednesday, I'd be given TTOs for the whole week. This would carry me right through 'til the following Wednesday, when I'd be obliged to report back to the hospital. Normally, for this week, I'd have to stay in the care of my family or partner. Otherwise, as happened only a couple of times, I'd spend the week alone. Even if I didn't feel completely happy during this time, I would feel safe – and this was the main thing.

Advantages of week-long leave

Week-Long Leave was great for many reasons. One

reason was that you could charge up your phone without worrying it might get broken or stolen. You could lay naked on your bed in the dark if you wanted without the nurses or other patients playing with the light switch (every room had a switch for the light outside the door, so staff could check you weren't in there up to no good). You could watch whatever you wanted on TV. You could smoke in peace and quiet. You could drink alcohol if you really wanted (never a good idea). You could order takeaways or cook something if you wanted. You could play Call of Duty/ videogames; use the internet. And in the morning, you could drink proper coffee with caffeine in it from ceramic mugs. The main plus for me at the time was that you could enjoy long soaks in the bath.

MY SECOND SPELL AT THE CLOSED HOSPITAL

No lighters

Smoking on my last stay in the closed hospital was only
allowed outside – it was after the law changed in 2007.
There was a yard area shaped like a rectangle, which
was about ten metres by twenty-five. We weren't allowed
to keep our own lighters with us, so during the day, a
nurse was stationed by the door with a lighter. He/ she
would then light our smokes when we queued up to go
out. At one point, someone smuggled a lighter into the
hospital. The mood amongst the patients was electric.
Soon, the nurses found out, seized it and things went
back to normal.

Crafty cigarettes

It was great just to smoke in your bedroom in the
hospital – mainly because it was forbidden. If you had a
lighter, you could use that. Otherwise, you had to be
crafty. While you were walking quickly in from the yard,
you made an attempt at stubbing out your cigarette
quickly on the carpet. If you did this fast and clumsily
enough, the end of the cigarette would still be
smouldering. Then, you had to walk with it briskly
through the hallways past all the nurses and back to
your room. When you're safe in your room again, you
took a couple of strong drags and the cigarette was fully
lit again. It was a good idea to have another cigarette
ready to chain smoke from the smuggled one. Then, by
the open window, you could stand smoking right in front
of it (so no-one else could smell the smoke). You could
even put on some relaxing music to play while you
smoked there in comfort. Usually, I just watched nurses

and doctors through the window coming and going from the main hospital.

Aliases

In the closed hospital, I bumped into a man there who called himself Bill. He introduced himself as Bill, and everything was OK. The thing was, I was sure his name used to be Carl. I'd spent a good while with Carl in the other hospital and I'm good with faces. I think he was trying to fool the nurses for some reason. He'd done nothing to upset me and he was known for his quick temper, so I called him Bill along with everyone else. It was a sharp reminder of who I was locked up in there with. I wasn't about to argue with him, whatever his real name was.

Judo roll on concrete

The yard was concrete except for a small row of soil along the four sides, where there were plants. Somebody had left a thin yoga mat on the concrete floor and it was red side up. I saw the red and thought I'd do a judo roll on it. The last time I'd performed a move like that break-fall was about twenty years earlier and on a proper floor mat. This time, I got it wrong. I remembered I had to have my arm above my head, but it was at the wrong angle. I managed to get up again afterwards, but the damage to my shoulder was already done. It turned out I had a rotator cuff injury. I firmly believed the colour red had compelled me to do it. I was furious with myself and the colour red - and in pain. It took months to fully heal.

The Gambian man

I was in the hospital with a tall, African man during my second time there. He'd come to England from a small village in Gambia. Just being in England was enough to drive him mad. For the first few days and nights, he was walking around the place dressed only in a bed sheet, yelling at people in his native tongue, Mandingo. He had a cassette with him containing music from his village. This was intended to bring him good luck in England and ease any home-sickness. His friends in that village brought his name up in praise in most of the songs. Whatever he wanted to do in that hospital, within reason, that man did. He was a force of nature. Also, he'd brought with him a big drum.

Raining money

Now and then, he'd ask a nurse if he could have his drum so he could play for a while. He was very talented. When the sun was out, he took his drum into the yard. He'd sit on a bench, put it roughly, yet precariously, between his legs and go about it. He told everyone he only played when *he* wanted to. He wouldn't drum for any other reason. Once, he was drumming in the yard and people started throwing money down to him. There was a smoking pod just above our door to the yard where the people above had to smoke. Out of the blue, while he was drumming, patients began throwing money down to him through the bars of their pod. He was getting tenners, twenties. It was amazing. He easily made fifty pounds or more that day – all in the space of about ten minutes. Even with this success under his belt, he stuck firm to his playing-for-fun rule. This was especially tested when the people upstairs wanted him to play an encore for them.

Serious Scrabble game

I have one other memory involving this drummer. There
were four of us all playing Scrabble while it rained
outside. There was the Gambian man, me, a female,
Indian nurse and a male, West Indian nurse. The two
men were very good at Scrabble. I was crap and so was
the girl. The two men would wait and wait for the perfect
chance to lay tiles as we each took our turn. Then, they'd
put all their tiles down at once, on triple word scores and
things. And because they'd laid all their tiles in one go,
they'd get bonus points for that, too. One game had
become so important for both of them that the girl and I
couldn't stop ourselves from laughing. Their focus on the
board rendered everything else superfluous. Things were
so heated on that Scrabble board that I suddenly had the
smell of burning wood in my nose. I asked the female
nurse if she could smell that too, and she could (this is
phantosmia, I was surprised to hear a nurse admit to
that). It was a battle of wits. It wasn't important who
won. It could even have been a draw but the atmosphere
was electric.

Flames and fried onions

Cookery was also available in the closed hospital, but
you were watched more closely. One day, we were
making hot-dogs. I elected to cook the onions. I know
how to cook perfect fried onions. The key is to make
them soft, sweet and translucent. Also, using hot oil, you
should aim to burn their edges slightly. Before long, in
that kitchen, I was in the zone. The onions were getting
cooked perfectly and huge flames were leaping out of the

pan. One of the nurses saw the flames coming from my workstation and got worried. I was a hazard. They took me off onions duty quickly after that. Then, one of the nurses cooked the rest of the onions. I was relegated to slicing finger buns with a blunt knife. Later, the hotdogs were officially served to everyone on the ward. Of course, people loved my onions the best. Sadly, my "unsafe cooking" was raised in ward round and I was banned for a while from cooking.

Comedy scripts

So, I had the idea that some of us should maybe read from some famous comedy scripts. Everyone thought it was a great idea and there was a lot of interest. We ended up reading scenes from Blackadder and some from Only Fools and Horses. It was fun, but in no way did it compare to real actors performing it on TV. Of course, the doctors were always told about us doing these sessions. The only main downside was that we were always more interested in smoking then acting. Even though the sessions were for half an hour, it was agreed early on that we should still have a smoke break halfway through.

Five-a-side football

One day, a nurse asked us if we'd like to play some five-a-side football. I really needed the exercise, so I put my name forward along with one other patient. The venue was to be the big, brand new sports centre quite nearby. The day came and cabs to the sports centre arrived for both us patients and the staff. The two of us felt like rock stars. Since there weren't enough patients for a full team of five, nurses made up the numbers. Our one and only female player seemed quite distracted when we finally arrived and kept doing cart-wheels all over the pitch.

My team-mate drops out

It turned out we were playing against mainly other hospitals like ours and I recognised some of the players on other teams. A few of those teams could easily have been professional. As for our team, my fellow patient and I hadn't kicked a football in many years. Then, with two losses under our belts, my team-mate threw in the towel. A cab was summoned and a nurse saw him back to the hospital. Now my legs were aching and I wished we'd warmed up first. When we'd arrived, the nurses all seemed blown away just being in the sports complex to think about limbering up.

I go in goal

I really needed a rest. I thought to myself goalies don't have to run much, so I said I'd go in goal. My first move as goalie must've looked strange. I stood in front of the goal and threw myself on the Astroturf floor, pretending I was saving a goal. I thought I'd be doing this a lot during the match, so I should practice while I had the time. It didn't hurt like I thought it would, so I thought I'd be fine.

Quite a place

The place really was state-of-the-art. There was a long, curving corridor leading from the entrance to the main sports atrium. Kids from nearby schools had decorated the walls with their arts and crafts. At the other end was the canteen where there were trestle tables piled high with buffet food. The football pitches were through some floor-to-ceiling glass doors. The Astroturf area was divided into four pitches by big, blue, blown-up tubes that were about two feet wide. There were narrower parts here and there so players could access the pitch. Sadly, we lost all our matches. Then, after all the running about and throwing myself on the floor, it was nice to spend some time filling and refilling my plate at the buffet. Then, I stood in the sunshine with the nurses and smoked while we waited for the cabs to take us back. I wouldn't sign up for football again, though, even if I properly warmed up first. My legs were killing me for days after that.

Internet rationed

On my second visit, I was surprised to find there was an Xbox for all the patients to use in what was the smoking room. Also, there was a PC with internet access. There were quite a few restrictions set up. Each patient was allowed a ten minutes (usually watching music videos on YouTube) under a nurse's watchful eye. Equally, if you wanted to type up a letter to a friend or family member, you could do that, too. If no-one was waiting to use it after you, you could stay on it for longer. Another change I noticed was that they held meditation classes in that room at other times. Since we were all red-blooded males, of course, the soft music, tea-lights and lavender were strictly to impress the doctors. Those sessions lasted for about half an hour.

I hit a policeman

Things were always tense, more so than at the open hospital. I saw a man I'd never met sitting in the lounge. He looked to me like a plain-clothed policeman. He was spying on us! So, for the good of the other patients, I went up to the man and hit him full in the face. I forget what happened after that, but I think he apologised. Soon after I hit the man, the nurses restrained me and talked me down.

Armani T-shirt

In the same week, I threw my arms out in front of another patient, really getting in his face. Oddly, I remember whispering to him quietly that he should hit me in the face. He then hit me in the face and the nurses talked us both down. Soon after that, I thought another patient had lied to me. He'd told me he'd paid £5 for his brand-new Armani T-shirt *I remembered this man from the other time I'd been in that hospital. Back then, he'd been covered in gold chains and jewellery. He never left the main sofa. He'd lie there, asleep, covered in all this expensive bling, but no-one dared touch him or call to him. This was a respected man. While he was awake one time, and thankfully, calm, we were talking about the news and I heard him say: "I'm in a dyslexic mood". I totally understood what he meant by this – only pictures would do.* Something about him struck me as odd. An authentic Armani shirt for £5? No such thing! I hit him in the face. He really didn't deserve it. The nurses saw everything, moved in and restrained me.

Jeremy blocks the doorway

There was also the time I was attacked while my Mum was visiting. She was brilliant, and always used to bring me the fresh olives I liked. I'd left the visitors' room to go to the bathroom. When I returned, I found Jeremy, another patient, blocking the doorway. I'd never seen eye-to-eye with Jeremy. At the time, I was still happy to see my Mum, so I ignored him and began squeezing past so I could get back into the room. As I did this, Jeremy hit me in the mouth. I couldn't believe it! I fell backwards onto a sofa. I kicked out at him from where I'd fallen but he was just out of reach. In a heartbeat, the nurses appeared and restrained us both. This was probably karma paying me back for my random attacks on the other patients.

Which men are you from?

A closed hospital was effectively one step away from the psychiatric wing of a prison. While I was there, a new patient, younger than me, asked me one of the punchiest questions I've ever been asked. He bowled up to me in the yard and said:

"Which men are you from?"

I figured what he meant was: "Where are you from?"

He'd put it in such a way that he wouldn't really need a follow-up question. What I said to him after that, any worrying, or any change in my actions, would all count towards what he thought of me. I told him where I was from, then began praying he wouldn't ask me anything else. Luckily, he didn't.

Practical and bizarre

The next day, I lent this man a dressing gown. I'd heard he'd fallen out with his family and had no other clothes, so I took pity on him. At the time, I somehow had two dressing gowns with me. I had a red one and a blue one. I kept the red one because it was warmer. So, quite dumbfounded, he accepted it from me. The logic was watertight, but the sentiment was left twisting in the wind. I got it back from him about a week later, but now it had a cigarette burn in one of the sleeves. I never asked him about the burn, of course, and accepted it back. The whole thing could've gone much worse. He always called the notorious Wandsworth prison by the pet name "Wanno" and he seemed to have associates all over the country. After his strong first question to me when we met, I really should have been more careful around him than I was. I had something he could use, so I gave it to him.

Pink sweater

One day, Alan, another patient, (on an all-male, closed psychiatric ward) chose to wear a bright pink sweater. People there never wore pink, not even purple – it was like an unwritten rule. People sometimes wore their clothes inside out, but that was as relaxed as it got. Alan sat down as usual at the lunch tables. This is when I started dropping hints that he might be gay, partly due to the pink top, partly because of what it turned out he'd done in prison, and partly because I didn't really like him and wanted to wind him up. Of course, intense boredom can make people act out in all sorts of ways – I'm never knowingly homophobic or judgemental.

"You know, there are helplines you can call, if you need to discuss your situation,"

"What?"

"You know, wearing that sweater. About you *whispered* being gay,"

"Fuck off!"

"Just sayin'..."

Later, with him still in the "offensive" top, I approached him again:

"You know, you may not find your soul-mate in this hospital, but I'm sure there's a man out there for you. Someone who, y'know, can satisfy your needs..."

This also met with hostility.

And:

"You're your own special creation, Al. Don't feel like you should pretend to be something you're not. No-one here will judge you..."

Just desserts

Later that day, Alan was smoking in the yard - still in the pink top. The next thing I know, he's run inside and squared up to me. I hadn't even seen it coming – totally lacking empathy, I'd forgotten how bad I was treating the bloke. The others must've been winding him up about my all my "homophobic" comments. He pushed me and I pushed him. Then (of all the luck in the world) I slipped and stumbled backwards onto the floor. Even while I was on my back, I continued shouting:

"Like a bit of man-on-man action? Alan?"

The nurses then restrained us and talked us both down. Soon after, Alan told me he'd hurt his foot while kicking me. I think he was trying to make me feel better. Not long after that, I found him again and proposed a rematch at midnight. I really wanted to face him again but he didn't show. After that, I forgot about everything and went to sleep.

Alan's arrest story

The main reason I didn't like Alan was because of what he did in prison. I just thought it was cowardly. Although he'd been arrested that time for drug-dealing, they'd put him inside for something else. His stories were usually about him throwing shapes and dancing in clubs all night. There was the time at a music festival when he'd swapped his usual ketamine for some LSD. The other bloke had been dealing LSD but wanted to deal in ketamine instead. According to the story, Alan had gone on selling LSD after that. It had been a great success, and made for a good story to share. Then, he told us he'd gotten arrested.

Fake paedophile

Then, he had what he thought was a great idea. Instead of the police thinking he was a drug dealer, he instead owned up to sexually abusing a minor. I'm not sure how the two could ever be confused but somehow, he managed it. He thought claiming to be a paedophile would give him an easier time when was put behind bars. Maybe he thought he was too weak to be locked-up with the real criminals? I think he just wanted his own cell. Still, I thought it was stupid and weak. Since my time in the closed hospital with him, Alan threw himself under a train and died.

Sour milk surprise

On the subject of paedophiles in prison, I found myself in a pub chatting to an ex-con, Mark. He told me regular prisoners hated paedophile prisoners and annoy or attack them whenever they can. The cells containing those sick individuals were right below Mark's cell. Knowing this, he got hold of a carton of milk, and returned with it to his cell. It was summertime and the sun was hot. Mark sat the carton of milk in full sunlight on the windowsill by his bars. The sun's heat soon turned the milk to yoghurt and before long, it smelled putrid. Mark took the off-milk to his cell door, and carefully threw it out. The lumpy, cheesy milk exploded on the floor right where the paedophiles were housed. They had to put up with the stink for hours after that. The prison guards secretly hated them, too, so it took longer than usual for it to be cleaned up. When you heard Alan (back in the hospital) talk, to mislead the authorities like he did was the best choice he ever made.

Jeremy hogs the phone chair

Coming back to Jeremy (the scuffle while my Mum visited) I didn't like him at all from day one. He was annoying firstly because he didn't smoke (everyone smoked), and secondly, because of where he always used to sit. It was the sofa chair intended for patients to sit in while they took a call from their relatives. Jeremy'd sit there just ignoring everybody. People would go to sit in that phone chair when their call came through - he wouldn't move. Those calls were like gold dust to us patients. He never seemed to get any calls, so he never allowed anyone else to be comfortable while they had one either, even if it was critical somebody speak to their relatives who can't come in.

Winnie the Pooh

Jeremy also hardly said a word and he dressed slovenly. His hair was always untidy with one stubby, fat dreadlock hanging off the back of his head. It looked like he had a turd stuck to his head. Nine times out of ten, he'd be sitting in that phone chair not saying a word. The patient with the call would ask him to move, but Jeremy would just uncross and cross his legs slowly and look the other way. He wouldn't move unless a nurse made him. We all hated him. One time, I'd just finished taking a crap, and he asked:

"Just had a Winnie the Pooh, have we?"

Sheriff fetish?

I found that such a creepy thing to say. If I'd had children, I would have made them keep their distance from Jeremy. He was probably the most annoying person I've ever met. Being a bit ill myself at the time, I would try and get under his skin. I wouldn't actually touch him, but I'd try and get a rise out of him anyway. He'd sit there in the busiest chair in the hospital, being rude, and I'd go up to him and whisper loudly:

"You have a sheriff fetish!"

The phrase didn't mean anything, as far as I knew, but I thought I was being clever using those words. I used to think the "fff" sound warded-off demons, and the "shh" sound made them quiet. It was the most annoying phrase I could think of. I suppose I wanted to dispel and silence his demons. Thinking back now, just the word *fish* would have done (the word containing both sounds) but I didn't think of that back then. The more I think about it, it was probably my antagonising that made him hit me in the face. At the time, as I've said, I couldn't explain my own behaviour, much less someone else's.

Love conquers all

While I was there, I thought I was in love. I missed
Gemma (the nurse from the hospital) so much that I
turned the other cheek with Jeremy. I knew that if I
kept acting up with Jeremy, it'd take even longer for me
to be discharged to the ward where Gemma worked. One
time, I'd been uncharacteristically violent on the open
ward. She was assigned to be my one-to-one and casually
blocked the doorway with her leg so I couldn't leave the
room. I loved the way we just kept chatting with her in
that position. She was so sexy whatever she did. I really
think I would've clashed again with Jeremy if it weren't
for the promise of Gemma. If I felt I was getting angry
with someone on the closed ward, I'd remind myself
about Gemma waiting for me in the open hospital. Just
thinking about her was enough to placate me. The two of
us would never really be together. Our whole
relationship was only ever in my mind and because of
that, I'd squandered the chance to have a fight with the
patient no-one liked.

Split-second fight scene

For some reason one afternoon, two patients were
arguing. Unbeknownst to the pair, a nurse was watching
everything unfold. Just before the fists started flying, the
nurse intervened. The larger man was just about to hit
the smaller one and it became a situation. In a
heartbeat, the nurse had leapt across the room and
overpowered the aggressor. Now, the nurse had the
man's face down on the floor, squashing his nose a bit
but with no bleeding. The patient's other arm was held
straight up with the wrist held in a lock at the top. The

patient's head was held against the floor while he was explained his immediate options. It all happened in the blink of an eye. And, although there was certainly opportunity for it, there was no excessive force.

Changing trainers

The nurse applying the wristlock was quite a vain man. He had a very stylish phone which was brushed aluminium on one side, which doubled as a perfect mirror. He'd look into this as he styled his hair, then return to keeping the peace in the hospital. He was an approachable person and, oddly, he always had different trainers on whenever I saw him. They could change even during the same day.

Nurse wears pink

The cat was amongst the pigeons soon after. This time, a male *nurse* was wearing pink – a pink shirt, to be precise. I got talking with another patient and we agreed how wrong it was for him to wear that colour to work. It was, after all, an all-male ward full of highly unstable people. This man seemed to be treating the place like a night-club. So, my friend and I hatched a plan. I'd approach the nurse wearing pink and pinch him on the arse. If I did this, my friend said he'd give me a 2oz pouch of tobacco – the biggest you could get.

I claim my prize

The first time I tried to grab Nurse Pink Shirt, he moved away right at the last moment so I had to try again. The second time, I made sure my friend could see everything. I pinched that nurse firmly on his arse.

"Hey! What are you doing?!"

He jumped back, shocked at what I'd done. My friend was watching from across the room in fits of laughter. To make it even worse, I tried to explain myself:

"I just thought that with a pink shirt like that, you... could really use a hug?"

Then I went to hug him but he pushed me away.

"Look! If you don't stop touching me, I'll suspend your visits!" When he said that, I stopped annoying him. About ten minutes later, after we'd stopped laughing, I scored my pouch of tobacco.

SOUTH LONDON

Banff to London with a thud

I had spent my gap year working at menial hotel jobs in Canada. I'd smoked a lot of weed because that's what everyone else did. Although I was living in the Rockies, I never once went hiking or anything else unique to the great outdoors. My family was right: I was strongly allergic to cannabis and psychologically addicted to it. All the stilted-choking, popularity-seeking lungfuls of weed smoke was coming back to haunt me. I was now helpless to a crushing paranoia and I still wouldn't quit using it. Basic relationships with family and friends started to break down. By the time I was almost back to normal physically (I'd lost loads of weight and my hair was falling out) after returning from my year abroad, I'd found a local dealer and the charade continued. Officially, life was a struggle too. One of the conditions of getting a work visa in Canada was that I had to demonstrate that I intended to return after my year out there was up. I had a deferred entry place on a Psychology undergraduate course at a major London university. Believe it or not, I'd forgotten what that would entail. All the other students already had an A-level in the subject so I was off to a terrible start. We were all made to discuss questions such as:

"What is a memory?"

And:

"How do we think?"

Everything is hyper-meaningful

The lectures that I did attend were torture. I couldn't

concentrate at all. I was distracted by everything: the weather, ticking clocks, sounds outside the lecture theatre. And why did my pen leak over those papers in my bag in particular and not others? On the rough paper the teacher handed out, why did the reverse side of it have pictures of animals on it? I felt overwhelmed by the whole situation. I would always try to lay low in lectures in case I was asked to contribute and revealed my ignorance of things. I was having (and hiding) panic attacks all the time which, of course, I'd brought on through weed use.

The "travelling stoner"

In Canada when I met new people, I'd tell them two things about me. First, I was always stoned and second, I had an English accent. My life story was that I was a world traveller who likes to get stoned. Nothing else seemed to be as important as that. I never said: "Let's go to the cinema, I love film noir;" or "Let's go white-water rafting!" The possibilities for real adventure were bountiful in Canada, as you can imagine. I was spending a year in the beautiful Canadian Rockies. This would have been the holiday of a lifetime for most people - menial hotel work aside.

Accepted by my peers

I'd never felt so popular! Whatever I said, my new, Canadian peers would typically say my suggestions or ideas were (the chicks) "adorable" or (the dudes) "awesome". They told me how they loved my accent and that we should celebrate with another joint. Back home in England, I'd always been a serious student with no time for parties, in Canada, I'd never had so many friends! I couldn't get over just how quickly these people would (seemingly) accept you. They used to call each other "cats" and spent their paycheques on weed or mushrooms. The "globe-trotting drifter" was an easy role to slip into, but I was forgetting my true self. I found the sense of there being an "honour among thieves" heady and addictive.

Fish out of water

So, I returned to England from my year in Canada a stoner with an English accent. Obviously, amongst other stoners with an English accent, I was nothing special. I tried hard to make friends with the other people in my lectures. I'd open with something like: "I went to Canada for a year and got stoned, it was great". Then someone else (usually male) would say: "I went to central London last week and got stoned, that was great, too!" And everyone would laugh. I'd laugh too, but inside, I was shocked to the core. I had nothing interesting to say. The rest of the group, as well as thinking how easy I was to put down, was even probably a bit jealous of where I'd been. At school, I had been quite quick-witted. Now, I wanted the earth to swallow me up. They all laughed at me repeatedly until I found a chance to leave. On my own, I'd mull over what a fool I'd become, why the world had become so cruel, and slip further into depression.

No snappy comeback

My laidback approach to life and lack of ambition had always worked in Canada. It was a dependable approach. Now, after the casual, early putdowns, I was drowning. I'd fall silent trying to think of a snappy comeback. All the while, I was regretting that I hadn't done anything cool and unique to Canada. Why hadn't I just once paddled in the Bow River, immersed myself in the Sulphur Hot Springs or something? During that whole year, I hadn't taken one photo. So, back in the group again, (after the "stoned in London" ribbing) there'd be silence for a beat or two while they allowed me time to provide a comeback. I'd let this time lapse - then keep lapsing - and I'd be wishing I was dead. This social, quintessentially British piss-taking never really happened amongst the Canadians I'd met. Now, I'd totally forgotten how to take part.

I'd taken my mind for granted

The conversation would then lurch forward. And I'd stand there reeling from the putdown. Inside, I'd be praying that they'd move on and that the focus would shift away from me. Occasionally, I hung around after I'd been silenced and try to laugh in the right way at their jokes. Then, I'd make an excuse and scurry off somewhere. In Canada, I'd somehow taken my mind for granted. God knows how my family put up with me. The long-term prognosis was: "weed rots your brain, makes you a zombie" but the short term was: "it's perfectly natural, Dude. No-one ever died from it".

Footprints on my car

Attending lectures took a great deal of conviction. Even if I made it to one on time, I still had to sit through a course I didn't understand. Afterwards, I'd fall apart again and eat my lunch in my car (a blue Mini). I always parked a little way off the campus, so no-one would see me. When I first started at the university, I noticed footprints on my car's bonnet which also led over the roof. It probably wasn't personal, but I internalised it like it was. I deserved it by because I was such a wretched, worried waste of life.

Dooming white

Somehow, I met someone and we moved in together. Now, I was getting stoned daily and often alone (as with alcohol dependency, a red flag that you have a problem). I was sure that everyone in the world (7bn people + me) was connected through a powerful psychic underworld. And I was the only person not buying into it. Initially, I thought that each time I blinked my eyes, every other citizen of the world was forced to register that blink – and came to hate it. I called it "dooming". If I blinked while thinking of the colour white, everyone would see white around their peripheral vision. Not only that, but when the colour doomed was white, they'd forget the skills necessary for whichever task they were doing. Surgeons would become vacuous mid-operation and remove the wrong organ. Airline pilots would become vacuous mid-flight and their planes would freefall (they'd not even understand what autopilot meant). And at a street level, car drivers would forget how to overtake safely.

Dooming black

So, everyone on the planet was affected by me dooming. All the skills people had would vanish instantly from their brains. Having no control over it, when I blinked and thought of the colour black, those vital memories and skillsets would come flooding back, returning life to normal. Obviously, the time when the professionals had spent wondering what they were doing between whites and blacks was a real problem. A plane can only nose-dive for so long before it crashes.

When seven billion people hate you

Directly influencing people's thoughts was a devastating ability to believe you had. People were crashing things and being killed right across the world due to me. I was worried and alone - in my flat, blinking my eyes involuntarily the way I always had. I even tried staring, just so there were less blinks/dooms. This didn't stop them, it just made things worse. I was killing people every time my eyelids came down. Before long, there were 7 billion people hating me (including me, truth be told). With every new doom, those still alive hated me even more. So, while I was sitting quietly on my sofa bed with all the windows closed, I started getting more and more scared of the world; more and more alone. Then things got even worse.

Dooming different colours

Just as suddenly as the black and white dooms shook me, different colours then came into play. The different colours meant different things, so emotions were being manipulated as well as memories. Blinking red meant people got angry. Yellow meant people got scared. Green meant people got jealous. Blue meant people got sad. Under me and my stupefying new abilities, the world became one big, dangerous hotbed of confusion and panic – all thanks to me and my eyelids. Of course, still underlying these new colour tweaks, black still signalled

remember and white forget. I was super worried now
because the whole dooming thing was out of my control. I
was playing with everyone's minds like bafflingly unkind
loner.

The Geographer

This fresh clutch of paranoias revealed to me one
supremely powerful enemy - The Geographer. He'd come
through to me and told me he'd given me the dooming
powers. This personality essentially was controlling
everything. He controlled life itself. He was very shady
and very charming. Tightening his grip on life was
always at the forefront of his mind. By now, I had
stopped attending the university and did no work. My
girlfriend was a gigging harpist and this was the main
reason I wanted to be with her. When we first met and I
found out she played the harp, I decided that she was an
angel sent down from heaven. Surely, it'd take an angel
to save me. We both shared a small flat at the end of a
long road. About half way along that road, there was a
bridge that went over some train tracks. At the time, if I
- by chance – opened a window, and the sun was warm
on my face or there was a nice breeze? I was made to feel
like this was a spiritual typo, an accident. I didn't
deserve such beautiful things. Even the smallest
pleasure for me was an abhorrence for respectable folk.
There was no love between my girlfriend and I, she was
a tactic. Always in my mind was the fact that the world
was happy(ish) under The Geographer's control. There
were all these people; plus me *at first, The Geographer
had wanted to rule the world with me, but I'd avoided all
the chances for joining him. All through my life up til
then, I'd had chances to perform a sex act against my will*

with one of his agents, but every time, I'd said no. This had happened so many times that, now, his patience had been exhausted completely. I'd wasted so much of his time, that now he wanted me (and, by extension, my family, too) to fail utterly in life.

My suffering to come

The Geographer would remind me of my suffering-to-come whenever possible. It was drummed into me that my Mum, Dad and brother would each be raped, tortured and killed. I was going to be raped and tortured as well but with a little difference: they'd never actually finish me off. The first time I heard The Geographer's voice was through the slow ticking of my girlfriend's travel alarm clock. She always kept it right by our tumble-down bed. It was so annoying. But I knew that if I took out the battery or moved the clock further away, it'd be like telling The Geographer to shut up. No-one silences The Geographer - even the most fearsome world criminals would never do that. So, through those ticking sounds, my nightmares dragged me further and further down – second by second.

Torment from everywhere

Years later, I learned that these ticking sounds telling me what to think were called "extraneous sounds". Even though they had been given a name, they would still return from time to time and they were still frightening. Over the years, I've been notified of paranoia via all kinds of sounds. Noises could influence which colour toothbrush I buy or it could prompt me to cross a fast-moving road just when a car's headed for me. Here are some of the extraneous sounds I can remember:

- shoes squeaking
- feet shuffling
- air-brakes on large, road vehicles (trucks, buses) releasing
- the wheels and gears of push bikes
- sounds of speech - from English, a baby crying or a foreign language
- balls bouncing
- gurgles and sounds from my or someone else's stomach
- skateboards or scooters clattering
- my flat's water tank refilling and dripping
- my PC tower clunking
- water sloshing against my ears when I'm swimming
- sounds of rain against the windows
- creaking coming from my flat's roof, walls and windows in the summer
- lawn mowers mowing
- dogs barking and yapping
- cars and motorbikes in the street
- fluid moving in my neck while I'm quiet
- coughs
- insects buzzing
- any of these sounds on film or radio
- cups clinking on saucers
- cutlery clanking while doing the washing up
- plates, saucers and bowls clanking when putting them away in the cupboard

There are probably also lots more I've missed. This paranoia could emanate from any noise, really, if I was stoned, worried or depressed to begin with. The best thing I could do when I heard an order through one of these noises to do something was to ignore it and keep otherwise distracted. It all began with the clock.

The insidious travel clock

If you imagine that each of these words took up one second, the messages from The Geographer came through the sound of the clock in:

"In- di- vid- u- al- se- conds."

It was like a drip-feed of evil. I was amazingly stressed when I heard these Geographer propaganda messages. This is just an example, but the timing was so focussed that I'd hear, say "put the pillow over your head", and the messages would allow me the time to carry out that action. Then, there would be further messages to me while the pillow was still in place. I couldn't tell my girlfriend because she was in league with The Geographer as well. She was a spy, plain and simple. At the time, I was even wary of Spam, the tinned food. Of course, the word Spam is *maps* spelt backwards, and maps would relate to geography, etc. Once I'd remembered The Geographer, I remembered evil.

Concurrent thinking

Of course, I was still dooming all different colours, now without even blinking. The world wanted me gone and the feedback from all the dooms just crystallised my fears. It got to the point where I'd hear different voices in my head telling me to doom. They'd say this just to wind me up. I'd hear "do a doom!" and I'd think they were focusing on my Dad (**D**o **A D**oom) and trying to get me to hurt him. If I managed to guess any one of The Geographer's plans for me before he'd actually told me about them, a shiver would pass through me. It was apparently evidence that I could think things as evil as The Geographer could, so I was no better. I'd hear:

"Con- cur- rent- thin- king".

You often hear surgeons on TV saying "I concur" to one another, meaning "to agree". When I heard this declaration from The Geographer, I was consorting with some of the most powerful and evil men on the planet, with the added threat that there was a reference to invasive surgery of some kind.

Conflict in Kosovo

At around this time in 1999, the Prime Minister, Tony Blair, was on the news a lot more than usual. He was always talking about the problems in the old Yugoslavia and Kosovo. The NATO sign was always shown behind the newsreader. For me, the sign was a clear message from The Geographer to his viewing public. There were four arrows on the NATO sign: pointing east; west; north; and south. This all tied in perfectly with my geography-fixation. Each time I saw that proof (that the prime minister was proudly working for The Geographer), my fears for my life and my family were increased. I even heard a hidden message from the word Kosovo. Whenever they said "Kosovo" out loud fast enough, to me it sounded a lot like "'cos it's over". I knew they were talking about my hollow life, which would soon be over. Of course, if I confided in anyone, things would just get worse.

Behind the green door

There was a weed dealer behind a green door nearby. It wasn't far from our building and I used to buy weed there every now and then. I never had a lot of money, but I could get a dime bag every couple of days. I was the only one who used this dealer with the green door. My girlfriend always said there were too many seeds in the bags you got there. She knew another dealer a bit further away who sold better weed. I'd smoke anything, though. If I got a crap bag, I just thought fuck it, I'm not worth the good stuff. I'd just build it, roll it up and start puffing away. I thought a hated man like me was destined to suffer and this extended to the quality of weed I smoked.

French/English bilayers

I started reading into what people said when they spoke. Some criminals spoke in ways that only other criminals could understand. They'd speak in French and English at the same time – French/ English bilayers, I called them. The English would be the surface thing you'd hear, but slightly beneath this would be the French. The French words would be the real meaning of what was said. An example of this would be:

"I saw a good interview in the paper today."

While they were saying this sentence, they'd also be saying:

"Nous devrions les attaquer maintenant, ils ne s'attendent plus à cela. *'We should hit them now, they'd never see it coming.'*"

Animosity builds

I thought these conversations were happening all around me. They were on TV, radio (pre-internet) and in real life. These criminals were mostly discussing and scheming against me. The feelings of persecution I felt at the time were incredibly strong. It was as if there was a contract put out on my life. People in my neighbourhood were all certain I wouldn't run, though. I couldn't make it fifty yards from my front door without freezing up with fear. How could I go further than that? They had about a week to plan and execute my abduction. In this time, they were collecting the world's finest neurologists, pain surgeons and other pain psychologists in one place – with everyone getting a cut. Whenever I wasn't tuned in to the vitriol of the ticking clock, you'd find me praying for death.

Living by one of The Geographer's bunkers

So, I knew for a fact that people were selling weed near my flat. Then, I learned The Geographer had somehow installed bugging devices all over the flat. The very next day, I noticed a door just to the side of ours. Immediately, I thought this second door was linked to the green door by a corridor which ran directly beneath our flat. My girlfriend had talked me into getting that specific flat because it was located above The Geographer's secret bunker. The whole thing had been planned so that I could be abducted one day and flown out of the country where my life of torture would begin.

Who's giving her money?

Sometimes, I'd be out with my girlfriend. I'd see her

withdraw money from an ATM and I might catch sight of her bank balance. It would have suddenly jumped up a couple of hundred pounds from a few days before. It didn't occur to me it could have been her parents (who were quite well-off) giving her an allowance. I knew better. She was being paid by the Prince of the Underworld, The Geographer. This really worried me. She was chatting about boring things with me all the time just to waste away my last few days before everything changed. Sometimes, she'd buy me weed or booze but all she really had to do was guard me.

Trapped within small talk

She had to protect me from people who could potentially give me a heads-up to The Geographer's secret plans for me – although failsafe suicide methods was about all I could realistically hope for. I was to be kept completely in the dark. We'd be walking along the street and she'd be babbling banter and small talk. But I couldn't concentrate on anything real. I thought all the time that she was speaking in French/ English bilayers. I knew she was telling all the passing pedestrians and drivers my secrets as we walked past. I'd be stuck listening to the English sentences she said. I'd be wondering why she was still harping on about the weather that morning when it was now mild and five in the evening. Also, I'd be thinking that I couldn't even get angry with her. I thought she'd start fake crying and people would attack me on her behalf and take her side. Then, I'd get abducted and thrown into some overseas dungeon somewhere. I hated those walks. I felt alone but I didn't have a choice. As far as I was concerned, *everyone* was working for The Geographer. These people were so loyal to him that any of them would lay down their life in a heartbeat. I thought it was pointless walking for no reason anyway, but still I tried to play along.

Zero Hour for the Victim

The way The Geographer put it, there was to be a Zero Hour. From Zero Hour onwards, I was to be constantly hurting (first, the careful removal of my eyelids, kind of thing) and kept alive so I should feel even more pain. The pain would be of varying types and intensities so I couldn't ever grow accustomed to it. I'd be known right across the world as The Victim – a deserving Victim. Uniquely, my torturers wouldn't want me to confess anything. I was to be kept in "pain for pain's sake" – no way out. They knew I deserved it. One of the main types of pain involved dragging. I'd be stripped naked and my feet bound together with rope. Then, with official sanctions, the other end of rope would be tied to the back of a Metropolitan police car. I'd be dragged through the London streets with people throwing rocks at me, or anything else they had with them.

Broadcast on TV

The police would have put out bollards and fences beforehand, ready for the event. Tens of thousands of people were expected to show. The route of the dragging snaked all around the capital like it was a Grand Prix course. The BBC were going to broadcast it on TV so people could watch me in agony pulled behind the police car. People would enjoy seeing me screaming with Zero Hour having been declared a public holiday. Everyone was excited to see me, the worthless wretch/ "Victim", twisting and turning as I'm dragged along the road.

After a while, I'd be bruised and bleeding with broken bones poking out through my skin in places - all before the baying, bloodthirsty crowds.

Cultivating hatred

My family would have been killed before Zero Hour, of course. They were by then just a loose end. All the people I'd encountered throughout my "pre-Zero Hour-life" will have all been secretly somehow working for The Geographer. This was so that when the dragging finally began, no-one would want to save me. People weren't allowed to even think about saving me. It was a test of how pure their hatred was. Hatred was an emotion to be cultivated. By this point, it was an established fact that there was no heaven. But The Geographer will guide you if you let him live through you in all things – he was like a reverse Jesus-figure. If you had a hard choice to make, people would often think:

"What would The Geographer do here?"

"How can I include hatred in this decision?"

"How can I force my competition to suffer more, even after I've beaten them?"

Rewarding hatred

Sadly, this selfish approach to life was especially important if the competition involved a family member. The lessons learned in childhood often stayed with you into later life. Say you stole your sister's doll and ripped off its head. Then you blamed it on the dog and the dog was put down. Your parents would understand this unscrupulous behaviour and then reward you for this. This was the twisted world the Geographer wanted.

Through manipulations of family members, blackmail and coercion like this was encouraged.

Psychic dollars

Along the dragging route, there'd be fences and police officers holding back the crowds. The fences were there so that the people wouldn't block the official camera angles. Also, there were special designated stops along the route. At these stops, the crowd fences would be lifted and the crowd was encouraged to attack me through the generous distribution of psychic dollars. Whenever I felt pain and yelled out because of a specific attack, a sum of money corresponding to the type and duration of that pain would pass into the culprit's bank account. The louder I was made to cry out or the more pain I felt, the more money that person received. The Geographer relished any connection between the real and the spiritual. He enjoyed destroying the sacred, especially if there was suffering and profit involved.

The Victim gets his world tour

Of course, The Geographer could also feel what The Victim was going through and ensured that whoever caused pain for him was paid well. Because of this gift, every psychic dollar was always distributed with pinpoint accuracy. Even the presence of a happy memory in The Victim's mind would lead to further punishment for him. And the Victim-dragging didn't stop with London. After London, The Victim was to be dragged, twisting and screaming through every major city in the world - from Milan to Mumbai. All the while, The Victim continued to be a source of income for anyone who wanted to hurt him along the way.

Evil exists to help us

So, The Geographer was a global crime lord, profiting
from every type of business - legal and illegal. He
invested in all types of warfare, right across the world.
He had governments put in place in countries which
didn't want them. And during peace time, he made sure
everyone was so worried that they'd buy things from him
– mainly insurance. He made money from the hurting
and killing of people, the jealousy and hatred of people –
every negative trait. All the while he was fighting
against anything pure or good. He could convince anyone
of anything. He'd famously stated that "evil exists to
help us".

The Geographer hates me

In some way, he prospered from each of the 7bn people in
the world. And they'd all been conditioned to believe that
it was a pleasurable duty for them to add to The
Geographer's purse. At the time, I hadn't realised this,
but I'd managed to hurt The Geographer on such a
primal level that he actually *hated* me. Everyone knew
that hatred was something The Geographer never
himself felt, it was just for everyone else. He liked seeing
people below him hating each other because it was more
fun than watching calm people. The Geographer was too
in control of his own thoughts. Now, The Victim had
become living proof that The Geographer was imperfect.
I was proof that The Geographer could lose control of his
emotions. This was unprecedented and he didn't like it
one bit. When The Geographer was tense, the world was
tense. Now, The Victim was to be made an eternal
example of.

Torture rooms and hospitals

When one of The Victim's arms or legs was torn too much by the dragging, I'd be taken to hospital. I wouldn't receive pain relief there, though. In much the same way that some say Satanic Black Masses take place under some churches, every hospital in the world also had a special torture room beneath it. Usually, they were big, largely empty rooms with walls twenty feet high. The room would hold all sorts of torture tools which were kept hanging on a wall in their designated places. There were big, blunt medieval weapons side-by-side with scalpel-

sharp, state-of-the-art precision things like lasers. There were things made to be put up my backside, in my urethra, eyes, ears, nose, mouth and no shortage of corrosive liquids. The room had a basic water and electricity supply and there was a simple bed right in the middle. Right before I was admitted to a pain hospital, I'd usually be teased by one of the first responders around me.

They'd reassure me:

"Don't worry, my boy. We're gonna get you fixed up,"

Then, they'd leave me there bleeding and maybe smirk as they walked away shaking their heads. I always wanted to believe they cared, but they didn't. They weren't allowed to.

Hatred genes

The pain surgeons knew as they went through their years of training that they'd one day be employed to torture people. The Geographer had selected them primarily so they could join his army as medics. Years earlier, he'd have united their parents to give birth to these medics, so they'd be just right for the job when they grew up. The Geographer loved people with a good amount of "hatred genes" in their DNA. Oftentimes, playground bullies would be hand-picked for positions of authority later in life because of these genes. The Geographer always nurtured these people wherever he could. He would pay for their training and cover their expenses all through their studies as surgeons. This would happen in tandem with the repeated, systematic physical and sexual abuse of the self-same surgeons. The traumas were applied so that any empathy was completely eradicated. Then they'd lead by example from that point on.

Paining-out body parts

The pain surgeons knew about all types of pain and every little way they could cause it *you could easily tell a pain surgeon from anyone else. He/ she'd ride a big motorbike, be totally covered in tattoos, and they'd have the pain surgeons' motto tattooed somewhere discreet. Most common of all was having the saying just inside their lower lip. This was a further nod to how no-one should ever mention the pain hospitals, at least, not without someone higher up mentioning it first. The saying was in Latin. It read "dolorum dolorem meum" or "pain for pain's sake".* These ways ranged from the mental torture of making someone fcel guilty or afraid to the physical torture of firing lasers up under a person's tongue. The surgeons knew all about how different forms of physical pain could be cultivated and sustained. Often, they didn't want a body part to be hurt so much that it went numb, died or fell off. If that happened, they had failed in their job. Once they'd "pained-out" one leg, for example, they knew they had to stop for a while to let it heal. After it had healed fully (and their attention turned to hurting somewhere else), they'd come back to it and ramp up the pain there all over again. After a few days spent at one of the pain hospitals, The Victim would then be thrown back outside and onto the road. After that, they'd continue the dragging from where they'd left off.

Pain pushers

Footage of the torture inside these hospitals was like gold dust. One of the crowd-pleasers carried out by the pain surgeons was when they cut off an arm or a leg – a tiny bit at a time. First, they'd give The Victim a special drug which amplified any pain he felt – the opposite of painkillers: pain pushers. These chemicals would strongly capitalise on the pain being inflicted; wounds feeling like they were on fire. Then, the toes would be taken off, one by one. When the Victim's body reacted with any naturally-occurring painkilling hormones or the area became numb to the pain, another millimetre of the Victim's foot would be cut off to introduce the pain there. Then, attention would shift to another body part, and another tiny bit of my foot would be torn off with pliers, or hacked off with a saw or an axe; corroded with acid; burnt with a laser. Also, there was always dislocating joints at the hip and shoulder and then forcing them back into place again.

Orgasms when hurting

A lot of the world-celebrity pain surgeons were discovered in poor, third world countries. Here, they'd often been abused and forced to kill or torture others from a very young age. The hatred had to be so strong within them that they could think of nothing else. They grew euphoric, almost orgasmic, when causing pain in others and they were always dreaming up new methods of intentional suffering. Under The Geographer's wing, these warped people would grow to become some of the richest men and women on the planet.

Harm is good

The Geographer was selling the world this basic idea (that harm is good) through all the available media. He was promoting a workable lifestyle. Alongside the very real discomfort I was suffering, there was also the propaganda machine. The idea was that anyone I'd met in the past (before Zero Hour) would have their memory of that past sanitised. I wanted everyone to get along and ignore The Geographer. I was effectively an anti-Satanic crusader for God. I wanted all the wars in the world to stop, for resources to be available for everybody equally and for people across the world to truly unite. In the current climate of fear and oppression, where the best defence is attack, vengeance cycles dating back in some cases generations served to only perpetuate and foster violence and pain. I was branded weak because of my visions of hope and peace for the planet. Even though I spoke to no-one about any of these positive thoughts, any counterculture ideas like mine were quashed straightaway.

My past is rewritten

Of course, for having these radical thoughts (and not even attempting to expel them from my mind), I should be punished. It was by now a universal truth that I was a creature that deserved all the pain I was in and all the pain I had coming to me. I deserved to never be relaxed again. People who'd met me in the past were told repeatedly that I was selfishly delaying The Geographer's plans. I'd somehow chosen to not perform the secret rituals that normal people had to. I thought I was better. "Everything he touched turned to shit," was a quote from one person I was at school with. To further emphasise these failings, dedicated news and entertainment channels were created (using clever, biased acting and subtle, manipulative plotlines) to make everyone who'd never met me also think *I* was the evil one. People grew convinced through these means that my punishment was a fitting one. They'd show how I'd always been insulting The Geographer whenever I'd gone about my business and my relationships.

Character assassination

The channels interviewed my cruellest teachers and the most violent bullies in the playground (both groups channelling the power of hatred) and portrayed them as selfless saints and heroes. Winston Churchill once said that: "History is written by the victors." And it was abundantly clear that The Geographer was the victor here. So now, post-Zero Hour, I was still being dragged from (pain) hospital to (pain) hospital. Also, at the same time I was undergoing an exhaustive character assassination through many different worldwide platforms. I was being effectively being rewritten out of my own past. Any suspected support for The Geographer

I might have shown was glossed-over or disguised. Any attempts to comply with society were dissected, reversed-in-intention and broadcast. The Geographer secretly welcomed the opportunity for such international hate-focussing. As for the man on the street, striving to be in any way more hateful, it was twisted anger and bloodlust that he saw when he looked up. And when he looked at his TV, he saw me screaming through choking blood.

Attack The Victim and win a family day out

So, I was still in the thick of it. People would travel from far and wide to come and see me, then apply their own, often lucrative, form of pain. Day or night, people would gather and throw whatever they could find at my body as it was dragged past. Some people would make a day of it - they'd bring the kids along. It was commonplace for even a young family to gather up bricks and random objects to hit me with or throw at me. Afterwards, they'd see the money (through the psychic dollars initiative) drop into their bank account levied on how much pain they'd caused. With this money, they'd enjoy days out at the zoo or at a theme park – complete with water rides and candy floss.

Who can hate the hardest?

I'd become a scape-goat for any extra hatred or loathing that people may have felt. Hurting me was the best, and most legal, way they could vent this bottled-up anger. They didn't have to worry about anything like evidence of a crime, alibis or being otherwise careful. Some of the most painful times for me would be when I was dragged through poor, third world country neighbourhoods. It was a way for these dirt-poor people to out-hate one another and at the same time raise some money for food. They wanted to show the world and The Geographer that they could hate just as well as the rich people could and I was just the opportunity they needed. Some people in these poor countries may have found it hard to hate someone else just for the hell of it. This was due to them still (although never verbalised) believing in God the creator. They were really the last surviving truly good people. They had few resources, so they were often strikingly overlooked.

Caring people deserve poverty

Good people globally were fast diminishing in numbers. It was only through hating and importantly: being seen to hate, that they could make any kind of money in this new, globalised world. The twisted, evil gained power and riches; while the good, caring people toiled in miserable, humiliating poverty. The Geographer had control of everybody's hope for the future and he wanted to crush the kindness I had within me. Now, he wanted me to be some kind of science project and he always got what he wanted.

Excommunication

As you may think, any thoughts of feeling sorry for me or of trying to help me met with punishment from The Geographer's people. The punishments usually meant that those people were totally cut-off from everyone else in the world. They were fired from their jobs, their savings erased and their name dragged through the mud. Their friends and family were forced to ignore them and they'd slowly starve to death, end up in prison or dead. On top of all that, their souls were stopped from going up into heaven after they died. The Geographer was never short of power and a favourite flexing of this power included excommunications like these.

God's right hand man

Everybody knew about The Geographer's background. When he was born, he'd been sent down from highest heaven, where he had been God's right-hand man. As he found earth and the way people went about things, he adapted and then came to rule. In his wisdom, he'd found that throughout history only the most evil, selfish people succeeded. There was no return for you if you'd caused him upset. As I'd really upset him, the current, ambient sound of silence was to be switched with the sound of terrified screaming, which was often to be my own.

Bad tastes

Back to my suffering after Zero Hour. The pain surgeons started experimenting with me now - with the vocal chords in my voice box. They were looking for other types of screaming and how they could make me scream in different ways. By this point, all I'd be tasting in my mouth would be my blood. If I started to grow accustomed to the pain, he would already know. The taste of blood would then be replaced with worse tastes, like urine, vomit or faeces. There were worldwide contests in which people could suggest tastes and smells for me to have in my mouth and nose. The proud winners would be shown on TV and given cash and prizes.

Cigarettes following joints

Back in the real world, the relationship with my girlfriend was getting worse. I couldn't talk about the stuff I was always thinking, but I was too worried for small talk. We were getting stoned together, but that was about it. We'd usually just sit there in silence. I was so worried about the police breaking down the door that I began always smoking a regular cigarette straight after we'd smoked a joint. I wanted the legal smoke to disguise the weed smoke in the room. I was too scared of the sound of my own voice by now to explain what I was doing, but I had to. I knew I was being uncool, being ashamed of the "sacred" weed smoke, but it was really a problem for me.

Notable time stamps

At about this time, I knew I was in a bad way because I was smoking so much weed. But I thought that if I smoked even *more* weed, my mood would come full-circle and I'd return to normal. It was stoner thinking at its finest. No-one knew what I was going through. And things had hit rock bottom with my girlfriend. There was a small, digital clock on the video by our TV in the room (the same room, incidentally, that served as bedroom, dining room and kitchen). Whenever that clock changed to a kind of noteworthy number, my girlfriend would read it out loud. As the time slowly crept past, she'd say:

"Look! It's 12:34,"

And two hours later:

"Look! It's 14:14,"

I'd usually just nod in agreement, trying to figure out

which time the death squads would be rushing up the stairs outside to abduct me for Zero Hour. Then, we'd have been waiting for so long in silence that (out of boredom) she'd roll another joint. We'd smoke that, then I'd smoke my strategic cigarette and things would keep stagnated.

Parting question

There was a 24-hour convenience store right under our flat. They sold everything: booze; shampoo; newspapers; rice. If I felt brave, I'd go in there for milk, and say "thank-you" as I left. Nothing wrong with that, you may think. But the way I heard my own words enunciate was that I'd finished by *asking*: "d'they unc' you?" If you try saying that phrase out loud, you can see what I mean. I couldn't believe it - I hadn't wanted to say anything like that at all! I thought the "unc'" part would be interpreted as short for "uncle" - an older, male family member who looks after you. To compound my problem, I then found out that "o Zio" is Italian for "uncle figure" and it also has guardianship undertones. For me at the time, it meant "someone connected to The Geographer and his global gang of criminals". So, after I'd said thank-you and walked off with my milk, I thought what I'd actually said was:

"Do criminals take care of you?"

It crucified me every time – mainly because I hadn't wanted to say it. On top of that, it was really none of my business. I thought the shop owner would think I was talking about the Geographer's crew of drug dealers nearby. Soon, I hated the exchanges so much that I avoided going in there at all if it wasn't an emergency. I was being nosy, in a roundabout kind of a way. After the dust settled each time, I felt rude for a different reason. I'd asked a question while leaving and left before they could even answer.

Can't say fair enough

Everything I said came out wrong. Before long, I despised even the sound of my own voice. I also had a problem with the phrase "fair enough." A simple phrase obviously, signifying an acceptance of things. I wanted my mouth to say "fair enough," but I'd hear the words: "fear and love" come out instead. I consider fear and love to be the two reasons we do anything in our lives. If you do something, it's usually because of one or the other or a mix of both. When I heard myself say "fear and love," I'd be caught off guard every time. Then, as I'm leaving the conversation, I'm worried I might have thrown down impossible conversational gauntlet to the others. It was another parting question where no question is required or even expected! So, in the weeks and months leading up to me jumping off a bridge, I hardly breathed a word.

Biblical 1999

The fact that it was 1999 at the time was really upsetting me. I started worrying about what would happen at the end of that year in particular – the three nines doubling as upside down sixes - the number of the beast/devil. I was convinced that instead of Jesus or God coming down from heaven to reward his followers, the Devil would come up from hell and reward his. Then, I started to think of *myself* as this Devil character, but I'd deviated from my path. I thought that I'd passed up all my chances to do wrong and create suffering – as the Devil should. I'd failed to crystallise my evilness by doing wrong and being cruel so now (according to The Geographer), my future meant *always* suffering.

English/English bilayers

I thought also that people were speaking with underlings all around me. It wasn't just French/ English bilayers any more, it was much worse. Someone would say something, but what they meant was a totally different thing. Both parts of their speech would be said simultaneously. It was like the French/ English bilayers, but I was getting out a lot less. Now, the hidden speech had been refined to Innocent English and Honest English. To demonstrate, I gave people an example of what I meant out loud. My example every time was the same few words and it just happened to be one that hinted at psychiatric care. It was just like "fair enough" or "thank you," but I hadn't thought of using those. Besides, those two phrases had already caused me enough stress. The example I always gave out loud was:

"In thy care."

Then, I'd explain how it sounded like:

"In Nike Air," at the same time.

Then I'd be the thinking of the shoes, and being slightly impressed at how clever I was – which really was beside the point. Usually, I was met with a blank stare and then a hurried change of subject or they'd leave.

Hidden TV messages

So, I was getting stoned and my mood was generally anti-me. My angel was getting ready for college and on TV, channel four was showing a programme called The Big Breakfast. We always had that programme on in the mornings, they quoted the time a lot and it was generally a motivating programme. The hosts that day were Johnny Vaughn and Denise Van Outen and everything was "to camera". They were talking directly to you, like newsreaders do. At the end of the show that day, I felt motivated in a very destructive way. I heard a message just for me.

"You should kill yourself as soon as possible..."

The only sane choice

When I heard this command, I was devastated, although I kept up appearances for my girlfriend. I knew that if I didn't try and end it all, there'd be negative repercussions for my close family. Furthermore, if I tried to kill myself and failed, it'd be even worse. When this is your mind-set and these are your two choices, the decision is an easy one. If I wanted to keep my family safe, killing myself was the only honourable way forward to free them from effectively being hostages. So, my girlfriend left for college just before the end of The Big Breakfast as usual. She obviously hadn't heard the same message I had. As the credits scrolled up for the end of the show, I had only one option. I'll jump off the railway bridge on our road. It was a clear day. It was around 9:05 a.m. And it was February 1st 1999.

Standing on the bridge

I remember seeing two cyclists ride past me as I approached the bridge. Two of anything indicated acknowledgement for me. The suicidal command through the TV coming on the first of the *second* month just made it worse. The bridge had quite high walls, probably to discourage people jumping off it. After I saw the cyclists go past, I quickly got myself up and onto the wall. There were no other people around that I could see. I didn't want people to try and stop me, like they do sometimes in films. I stood up full height on that wall for a moment, preparing to jump off. In front of me was a 35-foot drop onto the train tracks. I looked past the tips of my trainers and onto the tracks below. My plan was to dive off head first. As the top part of me started to fall forward off that bridge, something inside me changed my mind. I somehow straightened up a bit and fell towards the tracks instead feet first. That last-minute rethink probably saved my life.

Hitting the tracks

The train tracks rushed up towards me as I fell. I hit the ground with a loud, bone-crunching sound. Then, I lay there all twisted, broken and bent out of shape. I'd landed right between a set of rails. I heard a sound and raised my head - there was a train headed straight for me. Somehow, I rolled out of the way of the train, but only just. I was still paranoid. I was thinking: The Geographer will be furious with me now. He'll probably give me some time to reacclimatise, then he'll get to work hurting my family.

Commuters upset

Because I'd rolled out the way of the train, the train driver had enough room to come to a halt. The next station wasn't far away and before I knew it, I was being loaded onto a stretcher by two first responders. As they carried me past the length of the train which nearly hit me, my nightmares started again. I could sense the commuters on the train thinking at me:

"That's him? He's nothing. He thinks he's smarter than The Geographer? He thinks he can really kill himself? He'll never get the go-ahead for that, especially not now he's fucked it up."

And others would be thinking:

"He's making me late for work. They should just start the torturing now, do us all a favour."

"See if that was me, I would've jumped off head first. You know it's gonna work head first."

"I can't wait to hear that boy screaming in pain. No-one has ever liked him. The stupid prick." If this had all happened during the age of cameraphones, I'd have been recorded in my slumped, twisted, disposable shape being carried along the tracks. Any prospects of privacy would have been completely violated.

Rested twice on the floor

Whenever I'm in a nightmare, I can get carried away with the slightest detail. The smallest thing can catch me totally off guard. An example of this came when the ambulance people rested me on the floor twice (there was another number two again) before we got to the ambulance. They'd parked near the next station, and it was quite a long way there. For me, the fact that they'd stopped a total of two times was proof they were all quietly taking the piss out of me. If numbers mean anything, then the number two means two thumbs up. "I agree with what you're saying," kind of thing. I could tell that those first responders hated rescuing me.

Telepathic insults

In my head I was thinking: "I bet if all these commuters weren't watching, they'd leave me alone on the tracks to just get hit by another train. That'd finish me off for good. No-one'd miss me." I started thinking that my family hated me. They'd always known deep down that I'd cause them to be hurt. So, although I wanted to save them, I thought they hated me. Now, of course, it's clear that my mental problems all stemmed from smoking cannabis. But at the time, I hadn't seen this link and I clung to it like it was my only salvation.

Ambulance ride

The ambulance sped to the hospital under blue lights but I was silently terrified. One of the ambulance crew tried to make small talk on the journey, which was nice. But I thought he was speaking in French/English bilayers with underlings and so couldn't trust him. I genuinely thought I was being transferred to a dungeon somewhere to be tortured and that I'd never see the sunshine again. What happened was that I was checked into an orthopaedic ward. The other patients all looked to be at least eighty years old and they all had different back complaints. I was admitted there because it turned out I'd broken mine.

Fitted for a plaster cast

The first thing they did was to fit me with a plaster-cast. I was told to push out my stomach as far as I could, so the plaster wouldn't set so tightly it inhibited breathing. I interpreted this as a crucial test of some sort and pushed out my stomach as far as was possible. So, with my stomach forced out like a bloated Buddha statue, I had lots of wet plaster of Paris wrapped around me. I was preserved in that position for several weeks. It turned out that I'd broken one lower vertebra in my back, crushed another one and broken two bones in my foot. I must've really looked ridiculous in the pot-bellied cast – I couldn't summon the strength to look in a mirror. I could rest magazines and plates of food on my stomach where it ballooned out.

Creaky crutches

In bed, I usually like sleeping on my front or my side. But with the plaster-cast on, I could only really sleep on my back – I still have the scars under my arms from that time. The nurses and doctors told me to sleep on my back. If they walked past and saw me laying the wrong way, they'd tell to move – they could be quite bossy. Using the bathroom took ages but there was no other way. If it was just a piss, I had a sort of cardboard sock intended to be just for use by men. I'd piss in that and the nurses would replace it with a fresh one. If it was number twos I needed, I had to get both my crutches and hobble to the nearest bathroom. This hobbling option was painful for two reasons. Firstly, there was a lot of pain coming from my foot and my back, and secondly, there were the incessant creaking noises coming from the crutches. It was like Radio Geographer for me and I hated those trips. I'd even say that I preferred the physical pain to the mental. I was constantly hearing things like:

"You're a mess. You're a joke. It was mildly amusing, you attempting suicide. But your family's suffering is still coming. It's inevitable now. Remember: I don't need you.

We don't need you. Mankind doesn't need you. Your only
way up is down."

Sex within earshot

One night, still in pain but trying to sleep, I heard quiet
sounds coming from the bed next to mine. I'd seen this
man's family visit him earlier that day. He'd broken his
arm while he was doing karate, I think. Now, it was
around ten at night and the whole ward was in darkness
and this man was behind his curtain shagging someone.
As I heard her little yelps of pleasure, I was so jealous I
almost exploded. Then, I figured that the man was being
rewarded for his faith in The Geographer. It made
perfect sense after that. As well as it being a reward for
the man, it was also extra suffering for me. Two birds
with one stone for The Geographer there. He was
probably the only man in the whole hospital who was
getting laid that night and his bed was next to mine.

Dragged from my bed

The whole time I spent on the orthopaedic ward was
extremely painful, both physically and mentally. Of
course, I could never relax enough at night to sleep. I
thought that at any time, I'd be removed quickly from
my bed. It was inevitable I'd be bound and gagged and
dragged from the hospital by a team of commandos or
whatever. I'd have my big plaster-cast broken from
around me and I'd be thrown down the stairs and put in
the back of their van *I actually had some real-life stimuli
to support these worries. Every night outside my window,
I could hear the sound of trucks beeping as they reversed
for deliveries. (If I'd been at all thinking logically, I'd
have asked for that window to be closed.) At the time, all*

the beeping absolutely terrified me. What with all the underlings of words, the creaking of crutches and the sound of distant radios, the nightly beeping was something I could do without. It really didn't help the insomnia and the nurses were also bossy about sleeping during the day. I couldn't win. Every time I heard that beeping from the staff carpark, I was sure it was another hit squad. If they hadn't come for me that night, they must've come for someone else instead. I knew they'd come for me soon enough, as I tried to sleep flat on my back for less pain.

The Geographer said drink milk

The Geographer loved having orgasms. That man would climax hundreds of times every day of the week. He had such complete, psychic control over his businesses that he could afford to spend the largest part of his time relaxing or pushing the limits of his adrenaline. The two things he liked most were: sexual pleasure and inflicting pain on his enemies. Both were equally as satisfying to him. On the orthopaedic ward, a kindly, black *her skin colour is important here* orderly would come around a few times daily to bring us patients hot drinks. Although I usually actually wanted a coffee, I always felt compelled to choose cold milk. I kept choosing milk because that's what I thought The Geographer wanted me to drink. When you knew him like I did and saw evidence of his fear-driven empire all about you, you really didn't want to make him any angrier. Surely people would be more merciful after Zero Hour if I drank what he told me to drink?

They sip their tea

I was supposed to always ask for milk because it was a white drink (and it reflected my hatred for anything darker.) The Geographer wanted to embarrass me. I already felt frail and soI always asked for milk, which I'd come to think of as a Nazi drink. Sometimes I'd watch the older patients sipping their tea. I thought that they were paying their respects to The Geographer through well-timed sips. Every time The Geographer or someone else at his orgy had an orgasm, someone on the orthopaedic ward would sip their tea. It wasn't an exact science, but I knew I didn't like it. Each time I saw someone sip their tea or coffee (the drink I normally would have requested) I felt more like a pariah. I really wanted to leave that hospital and I knew I'd have to redouble my suicidal efforts when I got out. Jumping off the bridge had reduced me to a crumpled, physically hurting version of my former self. And now I was wearing a plaster-cast that encircled my whole torso from armpits to waist.

Threats from all angles

Sometimes, I'd have the small luxury of feeling bored. When I did, I tried to blow out my stomach. I wanted to touch my bare stomach against the inside of the plaster-cast. This was the most fun I could get at the time. There was physiotherapy, but that wasn't much fun. From time to time, I had the mocking, creaky noises of the crutches as I hobbled to and from the bathroom. And there were the nightly death squads with their beeping trucks, and the nightly, tinny nurses' pop music radio from the desk they manned through the night. That radio music was just a torrent of threats and insults meant solely for me

– the Victim. Sometimes, the night nurses would noisily shuffle playing cards while they were on shift. I took this personally, as well. I thought they knew I wouldn't complain or say anything, so why not earn extra money from The Geographer? There were psychic dollars available to whomever caused me pain. So, I lay there, really hurting, resigned to worrying about my family and the future.

Great hospital food

On the face of things, the day nurses at the hospital were top notch. One of the best parts of the day was when the menu was passed round for dinner that evening. It was great that we got to choose what we wanted to eat. There were always great things like chicken and rice, plantain, lamb curry, fish and chips, jam roly-poly, custard and sponge pudding. Once you'd chosen which meal you wanted, you then chose the size of the meal: small, medium or large. At the time, every extra day alive was a surprise blessing, so I always went for the largest portions. I thought I'd go out in style. Then, later, your meal would appear. You arranged the little bedside table in front of you where you could then slowly eat your fill.

Why not overeat?

Due to my dinnertime choices and lack of exercise, I gained about two stone in six weeks. I started thinking there must be a mix-up somewhere with The Geographer because I was still alive. I figured I might as well get dragged out of bed and meet Zero Hour with a belly full of food. Whenever I allowed myself to think that, though, I then felt sorry for whoever was being tortured before me. I knew that every night the beeping trucks took someone else away. If it wasn't that, then I'd worry about how my own family's downfall would happen. On top of these problems, there was the guilt I felt because I wasn't yet properly suffering.

I put on a brave face

Every now and then, a psychologist would come to my bedside and ask me probing questions. I put on a brave face and told her I'd been pushed off the bridge by friends by mistake. I hadn't willingly jumped. We'd been up all night partying and we'd all started walking along the top of the rail bridge for a laugh. I told her my hopes and dreams were still intact and that I was mentally tip-top.

Back into the hornets' nest

In the months that followed, after I was admitted to the mental hospital, the psychiatrist said she was amazed I could disguise my mental ill health so well. She said it showed a great deal of nerve to dismiss questions of suicide like I did. Deep down, my first thought was to get discharged. Once I was discharged, I could then kill myself in peace. Any safety the ward psychologist could offer would be inconvenient and short lived. Those psychologists are trained to spot anything unusual like: do they need help? If so, what kind of help? And for how long? My doctor thought I was clever to cover my tracks like I did, but I don't think she could have understood the depth of my fear and depression. I thought if I was locked up for mental reasons, it'd be a long time until I could try suicide again. So, more worried and scared than ever, I succeeded in being discharged back to the flat I'd just left. This being the same flat that had driven me crazy to the point of suicide in the first place

Too scared to speak

I should mention, while I was laid-up in the orthopaedic ward, my family did come to see me a lot, some friends of the family, too. I was always too scared to speak to anyone, but it was nice that they came. Although I never vocalised my fears, it was always a shock to see they were still alive. I stayed quiet during those visits for two reasons. The first was that I was really stunned they weren't already dead. And the second reason was my internal house arrest. Even if I summoned the strength to say something like "fair enough", I'd hear "fear and love" and retreat into my silent shell.

Don't mention Zero Hour

My parents never mentioned Zero Hour to me because The Geographer had expressly forbidden them. I would have bet all the money in the world on the fact that once the death squads finally came, that was the tipping point. The next phase of my life would begin and this would further strengthen The Geographer's global stranglehold. He was quietly over the moon that he had someone he could make an example of. You mess with The Geographer? This is what happens (bloodshed, screaming, and psychic dollars). It was perfect for him. Also, of course, it would make him pleased to see an enemy (someone who refused to live a life of hatred) suffer.

The palace of wisdom

So, I was discharged back to the little flat I shared with my girlfriend. Almost the next day, once the girlfriend was at college, I was considering instruments of death again. I thought if I was back at my Mum's house, she'd be watching and it'd be impossible to try anything there. I had a quote in my head. The English writer, William Blake, had once said:

"Excess leads to the palace of wisdom".

It was probably just a throwaway aphorism at a party, but to me back then, it was the only way to live.

What happens in Vegas

While I'm on the subject of sayings, "living for tonight" is really just a slogan the breweries use to make you buy their alcohol. It's like people who say, "What happens in Vegas stays in Vegas," and they swap "Vegas" with "holiday" or "on tour" or pretty much anywhere else. All that stuff while you were on holiday is still going to be true. The sad reality is that, actually, Las Vegas is where a lot of people go to die. They blow all their money gambling and getting drunk and shagging prostitutes. Then, they pull out a gun and blow their brains out. This happens quite a lot out there. When someone dies in a casino, the carpet the body falls on is carefully cut out. This bloodstained carpet is quickly and efficiently wrapped up 'round the body, then a new piece of carpet is carefully crafted back into the floor. I've heard they can remove a dead body like this in about an hour. Actually dying and your soul leaving your body in Vegas is the only real way something's going to stay in Vegas.

Suicide attempt number two

My official second suicide attempt involved painkillers and booze. I'd heard that if you took enough strong painkillers with enough alcohol, chances were: you'd die. I'd also heard that you had to buy the pills from a different chemist shops, so they didn't realise your plans. While my girlfriend was out at college one day, I slowly hobbled, with my creaky crutches, around all the local chemists I could find. Before long, I had a bag full of hundreds of painkillers and some alcohol.

Getting painkillers on crutches

All the while, there was all the hatred coming from the extraneous sounds of my crutches. I was jealous of passers-by who could dismiss the noises as just creaks. To me, at the time, it was a perpetual orchestra of hatred, mockery and foreboding – the sounds forming the backbone of the macabre case against me. The creaks of the crutches would be telling me things like "you stink," "no one's ever liked you," "hurry up and kill yourself... properly this time, you mug." That sort of thing. I remember also thinking I could feel the looks of hatred and evil coming from everyone I saw as I creaked and hobbled past. They must have known what I was planning with my bag full of pills. Then, deep down, they probably thought I might as well try suicide again - it'd save a lot of fuss later on. When Zero Hour is constantly just around the corner, there's a great deal of pressure on you to pull a fast one and take your own life. Every second counts when this is how you're living. I think most people, if their fears were as tangible as mine, they too, would've seen suicide as the lesser of two evils.

Interview with the Vampire

After about half an hour buying up all the things I needed, I had five boxes of the strongest painkillers you could get over the counter. I would have bought more, but people were reading my thoughts everywhere I went and they wanted me to stay alive for Zero Hour. The Geographer wanted me alive and well and he always got what he wanted. Because I was only buying a couple of packs at a time, the chemists were happy to recommend the strongest painkillers. I also bought some vodka. To coincide with all the suicidal thinking, I also rented Interview with the Vampire. I thought it'd be ironic. I'd quietly surrender my life while watching a film about immortals. And by the time the credits rolled, I'd be dead.

Black moments

On top of all these hassles, I could sometimes feel my stomach shaking like part of me was laughing. It was The Geographer laughing through me and at me. It was unnerving and made my mood worsen. Through the ticking sounds from my girlfriend's little clock, news came through that I had another black moment. Black moments only happened once every few years for most people. Some people never even had one. If you tried killing yourself during a black moment, you'd be successful. It was known that you had about fifteen minutes from the time the black moment was announced – my first had been during morning TV. Most people didn't need any more than one black moment to successfully take their own life.

Gold and diamond moments

There were other coloured moments, of course. The other two main ones meant great things, they were golden moments and diamond moments. If you were told you were having a golden moment – it was brilliant news. If you fully committed yourself to doing something outside your normal routine (with all your "heart and soul," this was the crucial phrase) you'd be made for life. If it was a diamond moment, the news was even better than that. If you acted against your normal routine in some way, you explored a whim, you and all your family and friends would be made for life. You could be collected from the street where you were in one of the Geographer's private helicopters and your old, trudging life would be gone for good. If you put your heart and soul into a deviation from your day-to-day grind and went for a massive leap of faith somehow, your life was incredible from then on. After a diamond moment, once you were safely on board the helicopter, you'd be told that all your family and friends had been set up for life in the most perfect of ways. All your enemies will be punished and you would even have a cushy place on the international space station if you wanted one and then up into heaven once you died. After acting on a diamond moment, you could do no wrong. Obviously, the golden and diamond moments were very rare.

Fifteen minutes

As for me, I was in The Geographer's bad books. I'd only been told about the amazing golden and diamond moments to make me jealous and depressed. Black moments were all I was going to get. At the time, I thought that it was just my lot in life. I was a wretch, I deserved nothing good. I used to believe that only inherently poisonous minds are capable of poisonous thoughts. Now, I believe that even a relatively pure mind can have poisonous thoughts. The world is so full of poison, who's to say where the thoughts originate? The ticking of the little clock told me that I had to put my heart and soul into my next suicide attempt. If I didn't grab the chance with both hands, I'd always be falling short if ever I tried again after that. After each botched attempt, I'd be promised even more pain than before after Zero Hour. I had fifteen minutes.

Serenity within suicide

So, I got back to the flat and began popping all the pills out of their blister-packs and into a bowl. I stumbled on a kind of serenity while I was doing this. It took a little while, but I was the most focussed I'd been for months. My plan was: swallow all the pills; drink all the vodka. I'd watch the vampire film, quietly pass out and my pulse would stop. At the time, I thought I was a bit like a samurai warrior. I was killing myself to save my family. It was the right thing to do. It was honourable thing. All pills eaten. All vodka drunk. I had a little of the black moment's fifteen minutes to spare. Lay back and wait.

Throwing up

What happened was that I fell asleep. My girlfriend woke me up, slamming the front door shut when she got back. Now awake, I felt ill. I went straight to the toilet bowl and vomited up all the pills I'd eaten about half an hour before. Part of me was glad to be alive, but another part of me was pissed off I wasn't dead. I managed to evade her questions about me throwing up somehow and life went back to how it was before.

House call

It was now that my girlfriend arranged a house-call from a local GP. I remember this strange man in a suit listening to my heartbeat with his stethoscope. He had a briefcase with him, with what I remember as being several syringes all lined up inside ready to inject. He also had quite a few small bottles, each containing different coloured pills. I only remember him coming that one time, so maybe I convinced him I was OK.

Suicide attempt number three

Another date in my suicide diary was March 22nd 1999, my third attempt. Things with The Geographer had stepped up a level. Living near the end of a road, you could often hear the high-pitched squeaking of cars' and vans' brakes as they slowed down at the junction. I took each of these extraneous sounds to be an insult. It was either an insult, or it was telling me to kill myself again, only this time, be more committed. The alarm clock was still spelling out my fate, too. So, while my girlfriend was innocently playing the harp at college, I was sitting alone in an oversized body cast with a broken back. Third time's a charm, I figured. This time I might be successful.

TV violence

It's hard to think of anything else when you're being bombarded from all sides. Every few minutes, someone new (through different sounds) was banging on about how I should kill myself. It was probably the squeaking brakes that did it for me that third time. I thought I'd try stabbing myself. In movies and on TV, the softest hit from a baseball bat can knock someone out or kill them. I saw a TV programme the other day, and the main character runs head first at a brick wall and knocks himself unconscious. People on film get run through with a sword like it's a knife through butter. Also, people's heads get chopped off easily in films. With all these fallacies of how easy it is swimming around my mind I thought I'd stab myself in the chest. My plan was to push the knife right through my heart.

Desperate times

The height I jumped from obviously wasn't high enough to do it. From 35 feet, it would've had to have been head first or nothing. As I said, though, something at the time had stopped me. If I was to stab myself to death, I knew I had to go in deep. At the time, all I could find in the kitchen was a small 4-inch fruit knife – my angel had probably hidden the other knives away. If I wasn't so swamped in worry about how the world was treating me, I would've left the flat and bought a bigger knife. I thought that the second I stepped outside the flat, one of The Geographer's soldiers would raise the alarm. Then, they'd throw me on the floor and the relevant people would be summoned. I would've bet anything on the fact that Zero Hour would have started that very moment. I thought I'd do the best I could with the small knife I had instead.

Desperate measures

Looking back now, the fruit knife had far too small a blade to do any real damage. Still, I pulled down my plaster-cast a bit anyway and put the knife point on the skin of my chest. I knew that my heart was on the left, so that's where I lined up the knife. What with all the weight I'd put on, the plaster-cast around me was now full up with stomach flesh and fat. I was touching the plaster-cast all the time without even blowing my stomach out. Still, the sharp end of the blade rested ready against my chest as my left hand held the knife-point steady there. Then, in the fifteen minutes after I'd been given a black moment (and with all my heart and soul) I thumped that blade totally into my chest with my other hand. The sound and the pain hit me at the same time. As the blade pierced the intercostal muscles of my chest, it sounded like I'd sliced through fresh cabbage. Once the knife it was in to the hilt, I twisted it to one side for greater blood loss. The knife narrowly missed my heart. About twenty minutes after that, my girlfriend arrived home. I couldn't tell her about my death wish because she was on The Geographer's payroll and she had to keep me alive.

New York massacre

So, I as languishing in the sounds of my girlfriend's alarm clock while she was at college. Four years previous, I'd been enjoying a gap year in the States and Canada – where I'd become psychologically addicted to cannabis. I'd tried peddling my stream of consciousness style poetry all the way in New York, where many thousands of strangers had indifferently noticed me as I walked the streets looking for open mic nights. Now, I was sitting in my flat thousands of miles away and was mortified to hear that The Geographer had struck again. He'd dished out thunderbolts (fatal heart attacks) to everybody who'd even *looked* at me back in 1996. I couldn't prove that it hadn't happened, but also, of course, I couldn't prove that it had. I was feeling very low already and hearing this news only exacerbated things. Those thousands of people had just that minute had their hearts stopped, wherever in the world they'd dispersed to in the interim. It was my fault for having been alive to be noticed in the first place. This new mass killing made me feel even worse because The Geographer had told their loved ones that it was my fault. And they'd been given my current address.

Intercom insults

One of my girlfriend's mates used to come to see her – no-one knew about me. There was an intercom by our door which opened the main door downstairs. People would buzz from the street outside, we'd ask who it was and buzz the door open for them. Her friend always messed around with this. He'd pick up the receiver in the lounge and shout swear words into it. We lived in quite a gritty neighbourhood and whatever you said into the intercom could be heard loud and clear outside. He would get the phone from its holder on the wall and sound a bit like this:

"Whoever you are, walking by this thing: fuck off! *pause* "Yeah you, fuck off, your Mum's a fucking slag! You're a c**t, mate! Fuck off!"

Then, they'd both fall about laughing. Meanwhile, I reflected that this must be how normal people behave and tried to laugh along with them. Inside, it used to scare the shit out of me.

Something's wrong

One day, my Mum came over, totally out of the blue. She found me rocking myself, curled-up in the foetal position on the bed – preferring silence. Immediately, she knew something was wrong. I was surprised and pleased to see she was still alive but I didn't say anything. I was still scared of (betrayed by) my own voice at this point. So, I thought I'd keep quiet and hope for the best. I was quickly and carefully loaded into a van, made to lay flat on my back on an old door and rushed to my Mum's house that day. I spent a few days there, then a doctor interviewed me and I was put in a mental hospital. My time fighting the illness started at this point.

THE OLD OPEN HOSPITAL

My first hospital stay

It was 1999 and I was put in a long-forgotten and derelict, old hospital. It was full of myth and legend and some celebrities had stayed there in the past. Apparently, there were underground torture chambers for the worst patients. While I was staying there, the psychiatrist said I had "secondary paranoia," amongst other things. This meant that I thought strangers were looking through my eyes and out at the world. These were some global elite people, too, judging by their voices in my head. They hated that I was looking at the tumbledown walls and ceilings of the hospital. They thought I was somehow trying to punish them in this way. Everything there was drab and torn. Furniture was usually ripped or stained. Tables had been broken but not been fixed.

Problems with the décor

Of course, I thought the Illuminati/Geographer's Brotherhood were seeing all this damage using my eyes. Before long, they were getting angry at me because I was there at all. Then, I started thinking I was one of them myself (early delusions of grandeur). They all thought I'd thrown myself into a bomb-site place just to annoy them. The secret rulers of the world were angry with me. Although I was told I was the most powerful in their group, they were furious with me. They thought I'd intentionally wound up in such a drab hospital. The voices in my head thought I was living there to spite them. These the people who otherwise live in the lap of luxury.

Do you play the piano?

The smoking room in the hospital was a very informal place and very dirty. There was an old poster on one of the walls for a ballroom dance that took place in 1982. There were a couple of long sofas in that room. There was one along each side of the room and at the far end was the TV. The first time I walked into that room, there was already one other man in there. We hadn't met. I asked him what I thought was a harmless question:

"Do you play the piano?"

Welcome to the ward

When he heard me ask him that, he exploded. Judging by his response, it was the last thing he wanted to hear from anyone. He flew at me with all his might. One minute, he's stretched out, lounging - watching TV on the sofa. Next minute, he's been asked a musical question and he's trying to kill me! There was massive banging as we both hit the door and a chair fell over. Then he started trying to choke me. There's no way he could've known me, it was my first day there. Luckily, nurses heard the commotion and rushed in to intervene. One of them took me to one side as even more nurses dealt with my aggressor. It turned out the other man was known to be violent, so the nurses pinned him to the floor and put a needle in him to send him to sleep. Tensions can easily build in places like that and if you don't hide those tensions the nurses can pick up on that. I think this man was an example of someone the nurses were watching and may have been overdue for an expression of rage. Either way, I was glad they dealt with him like they did.

The liquid cosh

The injection the staff gave to serious problem patients
was revered amongst the patients. We called it the
"liquid cosh". If you fought the effects of the liquid cosh
(if you stayed awake and insisted on causing the staff
problems) your respect levels would soar. They only gave
you the liquid cosh when nothing else worked. I had it
administered to me just the one time. For some reason,
I'd flipped out and the last thing I remembered was four
or five nurses all keeping me pinned to the floor. I was in
all sorts of different arm and wrist locks (and maybe
even a leg lock) so I couldn't move. It must've been a
sixth nurse who actually put the needle in. After I was
attacked that time in the smoking room, I was careful
not to talk about pianos around that patient. I avoided
talking about playing them, listening to them being
played, or even music in general while he was in the
room.

Ambient malaise

That attack taught me a valuable lesson regarding
personal space - both physical and verbal. Usually,
patients in this type of hospital can be extremely touchy
about things. I'd never been anywhere like it before.
Here was a place where you'd find yourself sitting in
silence with total strangers – while smoking, for
example. On the face of it, nothing was wrong. Often,
there'd be lots of hatred, jealousy and anger just hanging
in the air. It's strange, looking back now, how people
there could be both delicate and dangerous at the same
time; vulnerable and volatile. You had to give the worst
ones a good deal of space and show them lots of respect.

It was in your interest to do this often for your own physical safety.

Breaking windows

There was an old gym area in one part of the hospital. You'd think no-one had used it for years. The place had been left to gather dust - like the long, echoing corridors. The gym was also the furthest from the nurses' control room you could get without going through a locked door. It surprises me to this day that the gym back there was accessible at all for us patients. Any noise you made in that gym would never by heard by the nurses in their office. Nearly all the windows had been smashed. While I was there alone one time, I took it upon myself to break any last remaining windows.

Hitler reincarnated

One of the other men in there with me on the open ward thought he was Adolf Hitler, back from the dead. Turned out he'd read Hitler's book Mein Kampf a few times and enjoyed it. He did press-ups every morning by his bed. He also thought a huge Nazi army was coming. To hear him speak, they were soon going to swarm into the Houses of Parliament and take over. Unfortunately for me, he also thought that I was one of Hitler's chiefs of staff: I was Goebbels back from the dead. He wanted to scheme with me against the other patients. It was quite scary spending time with him; alone or in a group. The first thing he ever said to me in the smoking room was just one word:

"Emotion".

Bit odd from the outset, really. But, better than being hit

in the face.

Bedside scuffle

As it turned out, the Nazi wanted to play ping pong in the old gym with one of the girls (and African lady, not sure how that sat with his politics) but he'd found all my broken glass on the floor. He'd had leave with a friend that night and returned to the hospital rolling drunk. Someone told him it was me who'd smashed the glass in the gym and he rushed straight to my bed to confront me. Totally oblivious to the fuss I'd caused, I was half-asleep, dozing in bed. The next thing I know, my back explodes with pain. It was one of the hardest punches I'd ever felt and I wasn't waiting around for another one. I got up so I was sitting on the bed facing him and kicked him in the stomach (our Nazi link obviously unimportant now). He fell backwards, I grabbed his head and pushed him into a curtain which tore away as he fell through it. It was then that nurses arrived and broke us up.

Curtains for the beds

The living quarters were ropey in that old hospital. First, they'd make you spend a few days in an observation room. If you stayed calm and quiet, you got moved into the main male dorm. There were about ten beds there for the men and ten in the women's dorm for the women. The dorms really were substandard. The "bedrooms" were all arranged in a long, single line and each patients' private space was split by a blue curtain on a rail. Our rooms/ private spaces were about twenty feet by twenty feet. Each of us had a bed, a wardrobe and a chest of drawers. It wasn't much and it wasn't secure.

Short nurse rugby tackle

On one occasion, I was talking to a nurse in the dining hall. Suddenly, a patient ran past us. Right behind him was a second patient chasing the first. The nurse I was talking to was quite a short lady, but that didn't matter. She saw the chase go by and instinct kicked in. The lady dived at the man and grabbed him between the waist and knees. She held on tight, bringing the man crashing to the floor. It was a textbook rugby-tackle! The man's Walkman and cassette totally smashed apart like a firework on the floor in front of them. Then, he got to his feet and started yelling. He was angry at the man he was chasing and also at the nurse who'd floored him, breaking his Walkman.

Patients suing staff

Sometime afterwards, I noticed that it was the same old threat the complaining patients would yell. They always wanted to "sue the nurses" who had upset them. Someone or other had always "violated their human rights," but it was all talk. To hear that second patient speak, he was going to call his lawyers the next morning when office hours began at 9 o' clock. He'd make them come down to the hospital and fingerprint everyone, get DNA samples and throw everyone in jail. You soon got used to those kinds of threats but I had infinitely more respect for that nurse after seeing her in action like that.

Dirty tobacco smoke

Back in the smoking lounge in the hospital the smoke sometimes tasted different. I loved smoking back then.

Every inhalation of tobacco smoke tasted strange, but somehow in a good way. The smoke used to either make me feel angry or just remind me of how it felt to be angry. If I'd run out of my own brand of smokes or tobacco, I wasn't picky. If I'd been craving a cigarette for a while, I'd think nothing of smoking the dog-ends from an ashtray. If you found a box of smokes just lying around, they were usually fair game. Some patients left their smokes with the nurses, some kept them by their beds. Some kept all their cigarettes on their person the whole time they were awake.

Martial arts teacher visits

My favourite visitor, besides my family and girlfriend, was one of my martial arts teachers at the time. He walked around the hospital almost like he was gliding. He moved seemingly with no effort. He'd walk slowly through the different rooms in the hospital with me like he was floating on air. His speaking voice was calm, deliberate and measured. As he walked, he kept his hands behind his back. I was proud to know him and that he counted me as one of his friends. At the time, to me, he was like a real-life Jedi Master from Star Wars.

Charlie's feats of strength

I met Charlie in the open hospital. He could be fearsome when he wanted. It seemed that in London underworld circles, his Dad was revered. He was a shady figure but he also had the common touch. All throughout his life, Charlie had grown up in his Dad's shadow. While we queued for meds, he used to do the splits as wide and as low as he could. The others were scared when he did this but I knew he was just playing with them. You had to be careful around him sometimes, though. If he was bored, he'd pass a burning lighter across his forearm to burn the hairs there. The smell of burning hair would fill the air and he'd grin at you through the smoke.

Charlie absconds

One day, Charlie was gone. We all thought he'd been discharged, but it turned out he'd absconded. He'd somehow got out through one of the main doors, hot-wired a car from the carpark and driven off in it! Apparently, he made it as far north as Nottingham before the car's clutch gave out – effectively, the car had broken down. Then, he was arrested by the police and brought all the way back to the hospital in London. He was a champion figure for all of us patients when we heard about what he'd done.

Absent celebrity friend

After the fight in my bed, I learned to appreciate the sound of other patients snoring (quietly). If they were asleep, they wouldn't attack me. There was one flamboyant gay man in the hospital with me. He was quite a showman and his sister was beautiful. He'd always talk about how he was close to Boy George in the 80s. Apparently, the two of them had DJ'd in New York a lot and people gave them loads of free drugs to take. He was on the ward as part of a rehab programme from cocaine abuse and so was relatively sane. He told us all about how his "good friend Boy George" was coming into the hospital to visit him that afternoon. Every day, he'd try to generate interest. He'd tell us how he'd seen nurses putting the red carpet down for his famous visitor. It went on and on.

Told I can leave

So, one day, I was sure I'd been formerly discharged-ahead of schedule. All the nurses and doctors thought I was good to leave, so I thought, and I packed my suitcase. I waited patiently by the main door for my official escort as I watched other people going out ahead of me. After what felt like an hour of standing there and being ignored, I backtracked in my head. Sure enough, no doctor had told me out loud that I could go. I was gutted and, hanging my head in shame, I sheepishly returned to my bed area and unpacked all my stuff.

Conversations while inside smoking

Although I have successfully quit smoking for many years now, some of my best memories of life in hospitals involved just chain-smoking for ages. Before the ban came in to effect, we patients had the luxury of 24 hour a day access to the smoking room. We'd sit there for ages smoking and chatting, sometimes sharing soft drinks and sparing cigarettes for the others. We'd talk about everything: from breaking the law, to suicide attempts, to sex exploits and all the way around to what we'd do when discharged. One of the women there with me smoked Yves Saint Laurent branded cigarettes. She was well-spoken enough for those cigarettes to be authentic, as well. She let me try a couple, over the space of a few weeks, but they tasted just like regular cigarettes. She used to get a lot of visits, particularly from her grandson.

The grandson

The lady's grandson was a bit younger than me and full of himself. He boasted once about how he competed with his next-door neighbour with his music through the wall. If his neighbour's music had been turned up, he'd turn his up louder. Then the neighbour would turn his up even louder, and so on. The winner was the one who was playing his music the loudest. What I found shocking was how he used to treat his Nan. Without batting an eye, he'd go ahead and put his eighty-year-old Nan in a proper headlock – and walk her around the room like that. He'd humiliate her like this in the smoking lounge full of patients. Then, he'd start wrestling her, sometimes even putting her on the floor. I remember thinking how strange that was and I never liked it when he visited. Maybe that's just how they behave in a family that smokes Yves Saint Laurent cigarettes?

The walker

In the hospital, patients tried to keep busy doing different things. Usually, it was smoking and visits or leave, if you were lucky. When you didn't smoke, though, and no-one was coming in to see you, you had to think outside the box. One patient used to walk a lot. He'd walk along the long corridor to the door at the very end. Without cigarettes of any kind to look forward to, he'd touch the door and head back along the corridor and through the main hall. Then, he'd walk along the other corridor and touch the door at the end of that one. The whole journey one way was probably 500 yards. When he'd finished, he'd do it all again. Usually, I enjoyed finding common ground with the other patients if I could, to be friendly. I thought it'd be a good use of time between smokes for me to see what he got up to after walking through the hall, which was usually all we'd see of him. After walking those corridors with him a few times (and him preferring silence the whole way), I gave up and went back to smoking with the others in the smoking room.

Bad influence

That walking patient never put on any weight, probably due to all the walking. He must've loved the silence – he didn't even have music with him while he walked. Strangely, even though he did this walking alone all the time, when it mattered, he was more level-headed than most of us. When his parents visited, you'd see him get really angry with them. He was forever pleading with them to get him discharged, always articulately and accurate with his facts. He ventured into the smoking lounge once and we tried to make him smoke, quite light-heartedly, of course. Someone gave him a lit cigarette to drag from. He gamely inhaled that carcinogen-laden smoke and coughed and spluttered while everyone laughed. I remember thinking what a healthy reaction that coughing was. As a smoker, I'd had to learn how to handle my smoke, as it is with most smokers. It's quite a strange thing to do, really. Sucking smoke through a small paper tube must have occurred to someone like Sir Walter Raleigh as a great thing to do. Then for millions of people to do it in public, with other people joining in, with everyone paying so much to do it? Pretty baffling. Of course, after the first smoking lessons, I then went on to repeat the same thing day after day after that for years. No matter how expensive they became.

All-in with the pills

For my last official suicide attempt, I thought I'd go all-in with the pills. It was payday (Income Support) for me, so I bought up lots of boxes of painkillers from different chemists. I also had a week's worth of my regular meds, which were mostly anti-psychotic. They always made me sleepy soon after I took them, so I popped them all out of their blister packs and into one of my good-sized cereal bowls. Earlier that week, my friend had come over with his dog. I'd let the dog use one of these cereal bowls to drink from. Here I was, later, filling one of these bowls with hundreds of all the random pills I could source. I'd also got hold of the customary bottle of vodka, too.

Saved by the dog

I had before me my death equipment and I suddenly became very focussed. I was grabbing those pills by the handful and eating them as fast as I could. The sooner I was dead, the sooner The Geographer would stop threatening my family. Now and then, some pills would stick in my throat, but another swig of vodka soon flushed them down. Before long, I'd finished everything. I woke up alive the next morning. Could I get nothing right? I was feeling nauseous and disappointed. I came across some pills that were left over in another bowl. It was the bowl the dog had used earlier. I thought that his vibes on that bowl had somehow warned me not to polish off those pills as well. It was one of the most serious overdosing suicide attempts I've done. Who knows? If I'd eaten the pills in the dog's bowl too, I may not have been alive to see the next day.

SLOW STUDY

Must get stoned

When I went to Leeds to try a degree course in Biosciences and Health, I was leaving my family in London behind and going to a whole new part of the country. I wanted to start my studying life afresh. However, somewhere I'd heard that Leeds contained "the most criminal street in England". So, instead of going to all my lectures, I thought I'd get in with the criminals. And things quickly fell apart. Getting stoned soon rose to the top of my priorities list – addiction really is no joke. I'd been down the same path when I was at college years before, and before that where it began, in Canada.

Eyes go up

On top of getting stoned a lot still, I was also taking my anti-psychotic medication. I'd just bought the biggest lump of hash I'd ever seen. All the different chemicals in my bloodstream soon brought about some strange and unexpected side-effects. The doctors had never heard of some of them. The most dramatic side-effect of this time temporarily impacted my vision. Against my will, my eyes would float upwards. I had to concentrate to look downwards or to even just look directly forwards. I could only do this for a short time before they'd float back up again. Whenever I was attacked like this, I could only just make it down the street or across the road before my sight would be hijacked skywards again. Crossing the road was a nightmare. I had to heighten my sense of hearing so I was aware of cars driving nearby. The beeping at pelican crossings was reassuring because then I knew I could cross in safety. I couldn't look anyone in the eye during those attacks. I could only really look at their hairline while I tried to focus on what they were saying. With this to contend with, (and still not blaming the getting stoned) I couldn't have done any studying then anyway.

Method actor

When I got thrown off the course, I returned to London where I spent more and more time with my long-time girlfriend. At the time, I was worried about everything again, internally. I was back in south east London and I started saying gobbledegook phrases in a very plummy, very drunk voice. I was slurring my words all the time, but for some reason staying relentlessly in character. She'd say:

"Are you ok?"

"Whenever I open my eyes, little Buttercup, I can see my ears."

"If you don't talk to me normally, I'm taking you to see a doctor!"

"Why ever would something like that do something like you?"

I was so reluctant to speak normally again that she finally brought me before a psychiatrist and then I found myself back in hospital. I remember strongly believing that I could have stopped this posh charade at any point. I actually was being selfish now (not to mention hurting Christina) because I remember thinking it was fun to act rich and tipsy. Whilst most people would call it a day after maybe five or ten minutes, I dragged it out non-stop for days.

BACK IN HOSPITAL

Reassuring cycles

I felt I'd scored a win against the world, I'd tricked the system. Christina had no choice, really, but to do what she did. It was a very serious example of "living in the moment" being taken far too far. Ultimately, it was me who lost out – I once again landed in residential psychiatric care. So began another period of exploring the wonders of close range telepathy with other mentally ill people. Back again to sitting about with chain-smokers, competing with them by trying to eat more of the free food there than they did. All this is not to mention that my family had to suffer too. Forever demonstrating their loyalty to me while I reverted to type whenever I was alone again. I've been out for the longest I've ever been out now and I know what to avoid. If I've learned anything from my psychological addiction to cannabis, it's that: just because the cool kids do it, doesn't mean you should, too. Cannabis really can rot your brain.

———————

AFTERWORD

For anyone who is dealing with the life-changing effects of mental illness, be it first hand or otherwise, this honest and personal account will encourage you to see that there is hope.

My brother is one in seven who reacts so severely to the use of a drug commonly available in all towns and cities across the UK and beyond. I sincerely miss the brother I grew up with but deeply admire and love the brother he is now. I implore you to laugh at the funny parts and cry at the sad. More than anything, I truly hope you can learn what the human mind is capable of creating, fighting and ultimately overcoming. With the correct help and support, mountains can be overcome.

CONTENTS

Available worldwide from

Amazon

———————

www.mtp.agency

www.facebook.com/mtp.agency

@mtp_agency

Printed in Poland
by Amazon Fulfillment
Poland Sp. z o.o., Wrocław

49146161R00169